# The Battle of the Story of
# THE BATTLE OF SEATTLE

## David Solnit and Rebecca Solnit

with contributions by
Anuradha Mittal, Chris Dixon,
Stephanie Guilloud, and Chris Borte

AK
PRESS
EDINBURGH · OAKLAND · BALTIMORE

The Battle of the Story of the Battle of Seattle
By David Solnit and Rebecca Solnit
With Chris Dixon, Chris Borte, and Stephanie Guilloud
Forward by Anuradha Mittal
All articles © by their respective authors.

This edition © 2009 AK Press (Edinburgh, Oakland, Baltimore)

ISBN-13: 978-1904859635
Library of Congress Control Number: 2007939195

AK Press                         AK Press UK
674-A 23rd Street                PO Box 12766
Oakland, CA 94612                Edinburgh EH8 9YE
USA                              Scotland
www.akpress.org                  www.akuk.com
akpress@akpress.org              ak@akdin.demon.co.uk

The above addresses would be delighted to provide you with the latest AK Press
distribution catalog, which features several thousand books, pamphlets, zines, audio
and video recordings, and gear, all published or distributed by AK Press. Alternately,
visit our website to browse the catalog and find out the latest news from the world of
anarchist publishing: www.akpress.org & revolutionbythebook.akpress.org.

Printed in Canada on 100% recycled, acid-free paper with union labor.

Cover and interior design by Jason Justice:

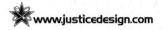 www.justicedesign.com

Cover photograph by Oakley Myers.

# TABLE OF CONTENTS

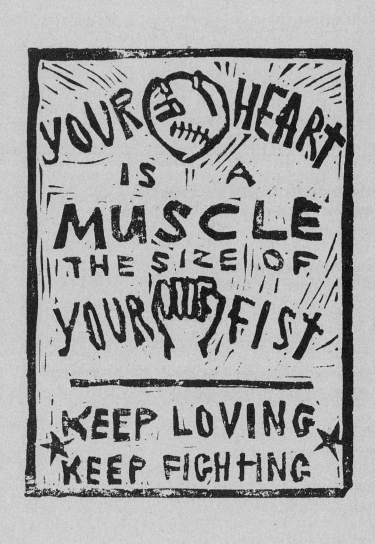

YOUR HEART IS A MUSCLE THE SIZE OF YOUR FIST

KEEP LOVING KEEP FIGHTING

*"I made this print at my kitchen table when I was twenty. The protests were on the radio, and I was bursting with the excitement of fall, and of learning to make prints, and the things I was hearing. I felt sure that every person actually on the street in Seattle stood for a hundred more at kitchen tables. The phrase popped into my head as the truest thing I knew, and the only thing I really wanted to say. It still is."—Dalia Shevin*

# FOREWORD

By Anuradha Mittal

It seems like yesterday when I joined tens of thousands of others at what has come to be known as the Battle in Seattle. Thousands came from all over the country to show solidarity and outrage, and more importantly, to make change. They circled the Kingdome demanding annulment of the Third World debt, while thousands blocked intersections, hotels, Washington State Convention and Trade Center. They were teachers, students, faith-based people, farmers, Longshore workers, moms and dads—and even turtles—who came from all over the country to express their disgust with corporate greed and its devastating consequences on working families, the environment, and life itself. They were tear-gassed and pepper-sprayed, but they stayed firm in the midst of it all till the front page of national papers cried out, "Talks Collapse." The world felt the tremor of this courage and witnessed a new face of the United States.

Events from November 26 to December 6, 1999, culminating in the shutdown of the World Trade Organization (WTO) Ministerial and the collapse of the trade talks, have been described many times over, been a subject of several documentaries, and even the focus of a full length feature film. To understand what transpired in Seattle, the Pentagon commissioned the Rand Corporation to produce a study, in which the movement was described as "the NGO swarm," difficult for governments to deal with because it has no leadership or command structure and "can sting a victim to death." Corporate public relations consultants Burson Marsteller published a "Guide to the Seattle Meltdown" to help its clients like Monsanto "defend" themselves.

The Battle in Seattle has come to hold a special place in political movements of the twenty-first century, and ten years later, efforts continue to explain and understand its true meaning. There are several factors that contributed to its unique place in history.

To me, as an activist of Indian origin, the significance of Seattle first and foremost lies in the fact that corporate and government leaders, along with their armies of bureaucrats, were faced off against young activists; trade unionists; farmers; environmentalists; anti poverty, hunger, and homelessness activists; along with street theater and puppets in the United States of America, a nation that is an unabashed apologist for unrestrained capitalism. Before Seattle, communities around the world had been organizing, marching, and rising up—be it the people of Madhya Pradesh fighting to hold Union Carbide accountable for the poisonous gas leaked from its factory in Bhopal, the ski-masked Mayan Indians that emerged in Chiapas to make the world listen, or the residents of shanty towns in South Africa who protest prepaid water meters as an attack on their human right to water. The mass mobilization that brought the WTO to its knees was carefully nurtured through cross border alliances, but was "Made in the USA."

Secondly, Seattle is an example of what strategic, determined, and disciplined cross-border organizing can accomplish. Its strength came from the diversity of civil society groups, and its unity from the diverse strategies they employed. The reasons that brought people to Seattle during the WTO week were myriad, but the tens of thousands of people on the streets represented the collective force of justice, democracy, and plain decency. What has been termed as the student-turtle-Teamster-policy wonk-tree hugger-partnership made the other WTO possible— the World Turned Out in Seattle.

And lastly, the blow delivered to the WTO in Seattle has been difficult to recover from. Once described as the "jewel in the crown of multilateralism," the WTO has come close to its demise several times since Seattle. Trade talks have stuttered and stalled and failed to move forward despite arm-twisting and blackmailing. It was only through the imposition of "war on terror" tactics—you are with us or against us—as was done in 2001, following 9/11 in the US, that the Doha Round of the WTO was moved, and has still to be concluded.

Doha was followed by the collapse of talks in Cancun. There, Kenyan delegates walked out of the ministerial, followed by representatives of South Korea and India, as civil society mourned Lee Kyung Hae, a South Korean farmer who took his own life to protest the WTO's devastation of the Korean countryside. He stabbed himself at the barricades built to keep poor farmers and other protestors out of the talks. Hong Kong followed, and the WTO had to satisfy itself with a minimum package that, at best, functioned as its life support system. Since then, scared by massive mobilizations and protests and the growing confluence between delegates of the developing world and civil society, the WTO has been reduced to having mini ministerials with the hopes of hammering out a deal with a handful of its members. Its credibility as a multilateral institution has been reduced to tatters.

The plight caused by the 2008 food-price crisis was exploited by international financial institutions, backed by the rich nations, in order to boost free-trade agendas and move the WTO talks further. However, efforts to promote the WTO as a solution to growing hunger were thwarted, and even the *Economist* magazine held the food crisis as the biggest threat to globalization. At a mini ministerial in July 2008, WTO members could not agree on the modalities to conclude the Doha Round, also known as the "Development Round," as rich nations once again failed to take concerns of the developing countries seriously.

In Seattle and soon after, those who heralded the end of the WTO and its free trade agenda were labelled as "anti" and called protectionists and even globophobes. The events since Seattle have proven that the international civil society that united in Seattle is *for* democracy, *for* livelihoods, *for* environment, *for* human rights. And that's what made it a force to reckon with—even hailed by the *New York Times*, on the eve of the 2003 US war on Iraq, as the world's other super power.

Seattle has gained new significance today, as the free trade agenda has shattered amidst the ruins of the global capitalist economy, and the few remaining tatters of the livelihoods and pension plans of the working poor. Seattle was a call to action for ordinary working people to stand up and take back their streets and their nation. It was a call to ensure that democracy is wrenched free from corporations and that it remains *of* the people, *by* the people, and *for* the people. Ten years later, civil society's vigilance and mobilization efforts remain essential to ensuring that responses to the current global financial crisis promote and protect the human right of all to live in dignity and to provide social and economic justice for all. ❧

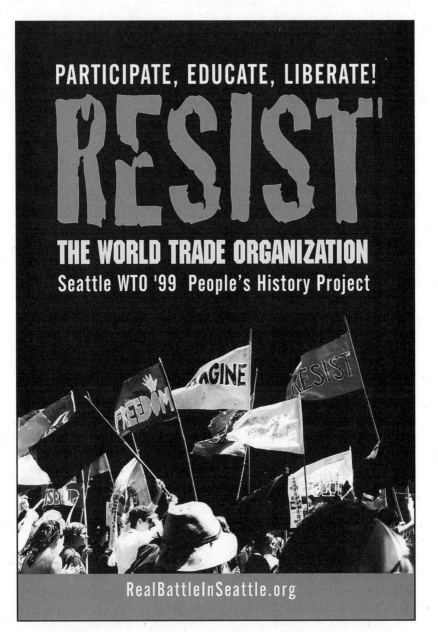

*Take off of the original Direct Action Network outreach postcard.*
*Design by Hugh D'Andrade.*

# THE BATTLE OF THE STORY

## Introduction

"Charleze Theron Joins the Black Bloc," read the subject line of Tobin's August 2006 email. He forwarded the blog entry he had read: "You know that thing in cartoons where someone sees something unbelievable and they blink a couple of times and rub their eyes? That's what I had to do when I read that not only was there going to be a movie made about the 1999 Seattle anti-WTO protests-turned-riots, but that Charlize Theron would star in it. The Battle in Seattle was one of the galvanizing moments of the anti-globalization movement, and it was one of the rare times I felt some hope for my generation. The film, like the event, is called *Battle in Seattle*." Tobin, a fifteen-year-old friend from the California Central Valley College and agricultural town of Davis, added, "I can't see it turning out well."

The 1999 Seattle WTO shut down and resistance has become an icon—a story that gives other things meaning. What people think happened in Seattle shapes what they believe about protest, direct action, social change movements; about corporate globalization and capitalism; and about police, the state, and repression. Stories shape consciousness. Consciousness shapes the future.

The story of Seattle WTO resistance has itself become a battleground. In the conflict, activists and movements fight corporate media, police, and government disinformation myths used to stoke public fears and justify repression against grassroots movements across the US. It also remains a source of inspiration for people hungry for positive change across the planet.

The 1999 Seattle World Trade Organization shutdown and protests had made a deep impression on Tobin and many other young, aware people. On the anniversary of the November 30,

1999 WTO shutdown, nicknamed "N30," he wrote to me: "Happy N30! Today, in 1999, while I was sitting in bed reading *The Lord of the Rings* for the first time at age eight, you were facing down the cops, and successfully preventing delegates from reaching their meetings. I commend you!" A couple years later, in August 2008 Tobin showed up at the police state that was the Republican National Convention protests in August 2008 and joined my affinity group. I did support with his parents (he was still only seventeen) to get him out of jail after the cops grabbed him for looking like "an anarchist."

I was living in Seattle and organizing with the Direct Action Network in the fall of 1999 through 2000, and for myself and many other activists, the event was a high point in social-change-movement organizing. I had been involved in many of the movements that fed into Seattle: anti-sweatshop organizing, Earth First! forest campaigns, anti-war and anti-sanctions on Iraq organizing, anarchist community and movement building activities, and the '98 and '99 global justice days of action kicked off by Britain's Reclaim the Streets and coordinated by the Zapatista-initiated People's Global Action. "Seattle," shorthand for the 1999 anti-WTO mass actions, was a moment when organized protest and resistance became a genuine popular uprising of thousands of ordinary people who successfully shut down the opening day of the WTO meeting, took over the downtown core of a major American city, and contributed to the collapse of negotiations that would have increased poverty, destruction, and misery around the world. "There were those who were saying they would shut down the city of Seattle, and they managed to do that today," Seattle Police Chief Norm Stamper said to the *Seattle Times* on November 30.

A few weeks after receiving Tobin's email, I got a phone message, "This is Stuart Townsend. I'm making a movie, the *Battle in Seattle*, and I heard you were quite involved." Quigley, a friend from LA, suggested Townsend call me. He later told me he did this because he thought I would push Townsend to do the right thing with his movie. I called him back and we chatted about the Seattle WTO and his film. It was clear that Stuart was very informed about what happened and also that he had not actually talked to anyone involved in organizing with the Direct Action Network (DAN), the central characters in his movie. He asked if I'd talk to his art department about puppets and art. I said yes, and told him I was committed to carry on the spirit and intentions of the Seattle shutdown. I asked to read his script to give him constructive feedback. He said no.

Once again, the meaning of Seattle was at stake. I was determined to do what I could, urged on by my friends, to do whatever I could to read the script, find out what the deal was with the movie, and see if we could make any changes for the better. The movie could shape what people think happened in Seattle, and the best thing to do was to try to impact the film before it was made, rather than protest or complain after the fact. A group of us organizers from the '99 shutdown of the WTO eventually dialogued and pushed Townsend to make the movie a little more true to the spirit and politics of the Direct Action Network and the global justice movements it portrays.

It was very strange for us, many years later, to be organizing together around how a past rebellion that we had helped to organize, was being portrayed by Hollywood movie actors today. We were fighting the very surreal "Battle of the Story of the Battle of Seattle," we joked.

We had actually been fighting this "battle of the story" since before the Battle of Seattle took place; fighting to get our stories and messages out through corporate media, fighting to make our actions tell our story in a way that was strong, clear, and impossible to ignore; and fighting to create and use independent media to tell our stories ourselves. And we have been fighting it ever since.

A year after Townsend's phone call I saw his movie previewed in Beverly Hills. Two years later, in the fall of 2008 his film was released across the US. As I write this, his film is out as a DVD. Townsend's fictionalized movie of "Battle in Seattle" takes on the elites' disinformation myth of Seattle, while it includes some of its own myths. In the big picture, the movie may help swing the public belief away from some of the worst corporate media lies and distortions, while at the same time re-enforcing some more subtle myths.

A different activist myth persists, in which Seattle was a spontaneous uprising, not the result of massive organizing, alliance building, and strategy. This misses the key ingredients that made Seattle effective:

a common strategic framework and massive grassroots education, organizing, alliance building, and mobilizing. In the essay "Black Flag Over Seattle," the best strategic analysis of the "Battle of Seattle" to date, movement researcher-writer Paul de Armond concludes, "Seattle was a seminal win." Years later, the US military think tank, the RAND Corporation, published an edited version of de Armond's essay in their influential (to military, business, and government officials, anyway) book, *Networks and Netwars*, and De Armond added a postcript that read "government authorities may have learned more from the Battle of Seattle than activists did."

Years after we had stopped intensely arguing and thinking about Seattle WTO actions, the story continued to matter. As the tide turned against the global corporate capitalism that Global South movements had fought long before 1999, the action in Seattle continued to be a major reference point.

When I edited a book on "the new radicalism" of the global justice or anti-capitalist movement of movements in 2004, I had decided not to include a single article about Seattle WTO protests. But it kept popping up. When I have traveled to Argentina, Israel, Palestine, Europe, or Hong Kong, "Seattle" was held up as a global turning point, often by movements who regularly organize actions bigger and more intense than Seattle. It came up again in January 2007, when the class action lawsuit against the City of Seattle for unconstitutional illegal mass arrests was won, six year after the fact. Many of us arrestees pooled some of the money the city was ordered to pay us, and donated thousands to cutting-edge global justice-related groups, including the Seattle WTO People's History Project, which was one proactive effort to reclaim our own history and tell it ourselves.

As I write this, ten years after the Seattle WTO protests, a global network of climate justice groups calls for mass action against climate change—the latest battle front between corporations and social movements:

On November 30, 2009, exactly ten years after the historic WTO shutdown in Seattle, world leaders will come to Copenhagen for the UN (CAPS) Climate Conference. This will be the most important summit on climate change ever to have taken place,

*International Longshore and Warehouse Union shut down all West Coast ports on November 30, 1999. Photo by Dang Ngo/ZUMA Press.*

but there is no indication that this meeting will produce anything more than a green-washed blueprint for corporate control of the world. We have to take direct action against the root causes of climate change during the Copenhagen talks.

Who has the power and resources to define our history and thus shape what people think? It is a challenge for activists, organizers, communities, and social change movements to fight for our stories and take seriously their telling.

## The Real Battle in Seattle

The real story of the Seattle WTO resistance is dangerous to corporations and governments, and powerful for people, communities, and movements. Of course the real story is the very different stories of the maybe 50,000 people in the streets, jails, and the many more Seattle residents who also experienced the week, who joined in or stood up to cops disturbing their neighborhood.

The Direct Action Network's "Come to Seattle" call read, in part, "It is time to raise the social and political cost to those who aim to increase the destruction and misery caused by corporate globalization, as movements in other parts of the world have. There is an incredible opportunity to use street theater—art, dance, music, giant puppets, graffiti art and theater—and nonviolent direct action to simplify and dramatize the issues of corporate globalization and to develop and spread new and creative forms of resistance. This will help catalyze desperately needed mass movements in the US and Canada capable of challenging global capital and making radical change and social revolution."

While we still have some way to go in the process of social revolution, the Seattle action did manage to act as a catalyst for significant changes, as well as a dramatic increase in activism and organizing. Thomas Kocherry, coordinator of India's massive alliance of grassroots social movements, the National Alliance of People Movements (NAPM), participated in the Seattle actions and wrote afterwards in his report to the movements in India, "The protest which took place in Seattle against the WTO is a milestone not only in the history of the 20th century, but also of the 2nd millennium. It is an indicator of how people's power will dominate the 3rd millennium."

In the days after Seattle I wrote a description of the actions for the forty-year-old anarchist periodical *Fifth Estate*:

> On November 30, 1999 a public uprising shut down the World Trade Organization and took over downtown Seattle, transforming it into a festival of resistance. Tens of thousands of people joined the nonviolent direct action blockade which encircled the WTO conference site, keeping the most powerful institution on earth shut down from dawn till dusk, despite an army of federal, state and local police shooting tear gas, pepper spray, rubber, plastic and wooden bullets, concussion grenades and armored vehicles. The Washington National Guard's 81st Infantry Brigade, 1-303 Armor Battalion, and the 898th Combat Engineer Battalion was deployed. People continued to resist throughout the week despite a clampdown that included nearly 600 arrests and the declaration of a "state of emergency" and suspension of basic civil liberties in downtown Seattle. Longshore workers shut down every West Coast port from Alaska to Los Angeles. Large numbers of Seattle taxi drivers went on strike. All week the fire fighters' union refused

*People climb onto and over the wall of buses used to surround and protect the WTO Convention Center. Nov 30, 1999. Photo by Scott Engelhardt.*

authorities' requests to turn their fire hoses on people. Tens of thousands of working people and students skipped or walked out of work or school.

People across the globe took action in solidarity. In India, thousands of farmers in Karnataka marched to Bangalore, and over a thousand villagers from Anjar in Narmada Valley held a procession. Thousands took to the streets in the Philippines, Portugal, Pakistan, Turkey, Korea, and across Europe, the United States and Canada. 75,000 people marched in 80 different French cities and 800 miners clashed with police. In Italy, the headquarters of the National Committee for Bio-Safety was occupied. In the period leading up to the WTO Ministerial resistance increased; an occupation of the WTO world headquarters in Geneva; Turkish peasants, trade unionists and environmentalists marched on the capital of Ankara; a street party shut down traffic in New York City's Times Square; activist's took over US Trade Representative Charlene Barshefsky's offices; and 3,000 workers and students rallied in Seoul, Korea.

Thousands of activists continued to engage in nonviolent direct action throughout the week, despite a clampdown that included nearly 600 arrests, continued tear gassing and police rioting, the declaration of a "state of emergency," and suspension of the basic rights of free speech and assembly in downtown Seattle.

The corporate media tried to dismiss a public uprising of tens of thousands that had tapped into popular anti-corporate sentiment, by focusing on the spectacle of a few dozen "black bloc" participants who broke corporate chain store windows well after the blockades had already shut down the opening of the WTO, after thousands had taken over downtown Seattle, and after the police had begun using teargas, pepper spray, and rubber bullets. The cops and politicians also tried to use broken windows to justify their repression and brutality. Despite this, a month later, in January 2000, an opinion poll by *Business Week* found that 52 percent of Americans sympathized with the protestors at the WTO in Seattle.

## WTO POST-SEATTLE

In the years that followed Seattle, global justice and anti-capitalist activists were energized as northern movements joined already thriving global south movements to challenge corporate capital's efforts to further concentrate power and wealth. In 2001, the WTO met in Doha, Qatar, the remote Middle East dictatorship, to escape confrontation by civil society and social movements. In Doha, just months after the September 11, 2001 attacks, rich countries used strong-arm tactics and sympathy for the US to shove through the so-called "Doha Round" framework for future trade negotiations.

The 2003 WTO meeting, in Cancun, Mexico, fell apart because of farmer-led protests outside and a rebellion of the poorer developing countries inside. The same year, the FTAA (Free Trade Area of the Americas) attempted to impose WTO-style corporate rule on the western hemisphere, but that agreement collapsed due to popular hemisphere-wide opposition.

The WTO meeting in Hong Kong in 2005 struggled just to survive, as local movement activists and thousands from Indonesia, the Philippines, and Thailand, along with 1,500 militant Korean farmers and workers, and people from across Asia marched, fought through police lines, and held sit-ins.

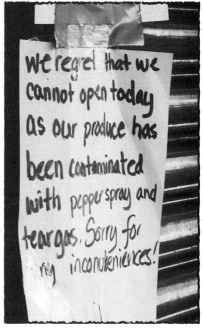

*Signs at Seattle Pike Place market after police tear-gassed and pepper-sprayed at the open air produce market. Photos by Kathy Whalen.*

*Photo by Derek Chung.*

*Street blockade of the WTO in Cancun Mexico. November 2003.
Photo by Orin Langelle, Global Justice Ecology Project.*

*Korean farmers and workers demonstrate against the WTO in
Hong Kong. December 2005. Photo by David Solnit.*

*All day thousands took over the streets of downtown Seattle.
Nov. 30, 1999. Photo by Scott Engelhardt.*

The WTO has become increasingly irrelevant and powerless. It is supposed to have a Ministerial level meeting every two years, but the 2007 meeting was cancelled to avert disaster. Elites, however, are trying desperately to revive the WTO. In summer 2008—using the pretext of the global food crisis—and again both in the winter 2008 and Spring 2009, the G20 used the financial crisis, which they were most responsible for creating, to argue for the expansion of the WTO; in essence, the argument hinged upon expanding the very policies that had created these crises and the accompanying widespread hunger and poverty.

Now the WTO has scheduled their first Ministerial Meeting in four years for November 30, 2009—ten years to the day of the shutdown of their Seattle Ministerial—in a last ditch effort to revive and shove through the "Doha Round."

## Powerholders' Myth of Activist Violence

"Protesters throwing Urine" is one myth of activist violence used by authorities to criminalize protest since Seattle, yet there are no documented cases of this actually happening in Seattle or at other global justice events. This kind of myth is used to create greater public acceptance of the curtailing of civil liberties and the use of violence and repression against protests and participants. Civil Liberties advocate David Meieran, of the group Save Our Civil Liberties, explained, "This is part of a spectrum of information war strategies that the state uses to repress dissent. 'Urine and feces' have to be understood within the larger context of the police's disinformation about protests and demonstrations. We've repeatedly heard the same language used in different cities ('urine and feces,' 'not your father's protesters')."

Since the Seattle WTO shutdown, police, government authorities, and corporate media have characterized major political mobilizations in the US and internationally as potential recurrences of the "violent riots" that supposedly occurred in Seattle. In the lead-up to mass demonstrations against the 2000 Democratic National Convention in Los Angeles, for instance, police agencies produced a video that combined images of activists at the WTO in Seattle breaking corporate chain store windows, with marginalizing clips of some Eugene activists who had allowed *60 Minutes* and other corporate media outlets to do extensive features on them as "Eugene Anarchists," as one way to help the public dismiss what had happened in Seattle. Police showed the video to the Los Angeles City Council just before a vote on funding a massive police presence and new riot gear to counter the demonstrations. The Council was scared, and the funding measure passed.

One of the most blatant distortions of the Seattle story is a report about the New York City Police Department's (NYPD) intelligence program, which attempts to justify the widespread suspension of civil liberties, mass arrests, and unrestrained spying and harassment that took place during the 2004 Republican National Convention in New York City. The report says that the history of activist groups "is one of extreme violence, vandalism and unlawfulness," and it links anarchists and "direct action specialists" to "extreme violence" and "terrorism operatives."

The NYPD's history of Seattle included completely fabricated references to overturned police and emergency vehicles. The report provides a long list of terrorist attacks around the world together with a list of international grassroots global justice, peace, and other mobilizations, suggesting the latter was indistinguishable from the former and that they were both threats that justified repression.

Another elite myth, put forth by pro-corporate globalization *New York Times* columnist Thomas Friedman and others, is that anti-WTO activists were naive and against all trade. As the actions in Seattle unfolded in 1999, Friedman wrote in his column, "Is there anything more ridiculous in the news today than the protests against the World Trade Organization in Seattle? I doubt it. These anti-W.T.O. protesters— who are a Noah's ark of flat-earth advocates, protectionist trade unions and yuppies looking for their 1960's fix—are protesting against the wrong target with the wrong tools." (This was well before his 2005 book on globalization, *The Earth is Flat*.) He was among the first to sound the elite backlash against the movements in Seattle. *Business Week* named it "Seattle Shock" and warned that Seattle marked a dangerous popular backlash against "our very economic system." When asked about Friedman's comment, corporate critic Noam Chomsky responded, "From the point of view of slave owners, people opposed to slavery probably looked that way. For the 1 percent of the population that he's thinking about and representing, the people who are opposing this are

*Nov 30, 1999. Photo by Lauren E. Sayoc.*

*Nov 30, 1999. Photo by Lauren E. Sayoc.*

*Police teargas and fire rubber bullets on blockaders as WTO is effectively shut down. Nov 30, 1999. Photo by Stephen Kaiser.*

*Police pepperspray blockades after WTO is shut down and opening ceremony cancelled. Nov 30, 1999. Photo by Stephen Kaiser.*

flat-earthers." As the corporate globalized economic system collapses nearly ten years later, even former US Federal Reserve chairman, Alan Greenspan, is calling the free market ideology a mistake.

More recently, references to "violent riots" at the Seattle WTO have increased as nervous authorities attempt to justify the suspension of civil liberties in the face of recent mobilizations at the 2008 Democratic and Republican National Conventions and the 2009 G20 in Pittsburgh. Leading up to the Democratic National Convention in Denver in 2008, a columnist in Denver's weekly paper, *Westword*, wrote that, "If 1999 put law-enforcement agencies on alert, 9/11 put them on lockdown. New anti-terrorism laws and programs gave them the ability to successfully quash militant protest groups, pouring millions into security measures that essentially turn cities that host large trade events or political conventions into militarized zones."

## Activist Myth of Spontaneous Rebellion

There is another myth of Seattle WTO: this is the activist and radical myth that Seattle was largely a semi-spontaneous rebellion or that it depended mostly on an element of surprise, or even luck. This myth overlooks the massive amounts of grassroots organizing, mobilizing, networking, education, alliance building, media work, and the creation of a unifying strategic framework. This is not to negate the unexplainable elements, like emergent intelligence—people thinking along the same lines at the same time, nationally and globally—that took place in conjunction with the strong foundation of organizing and strategy. The result has been a series of not-so-well planned, narrowly framed, under-organized mass actions that lack clear strategy or widespread public support, which have fallen flat, left their participants disappointed, or been repressed.

### LESSONS NOT LEARNED

In the year or so after Seattle, a coalition, led in part by the Ruckus Society, decided to mobilize against a biotechnology industry conference in San Diego. They adopted the trappings of the Seattle WTO mobilization—a call to action, website, convergence space—called it "BIO-Justice," and promised it might be "the next Seattle."

They even promised some activists stipends if they would come out and help organize. It lacked any grassroots base of support, education campaign, or real grassroots mobilizing, and when people came out in the dozens instead of the thousands hoped for, disappointed activists nicknamed the mobilization "BIO-Just Us."

In 2004, a national mobilization took place in New York City to protest the Republican National Convention. One group of organizers took on coordinating a nonviolent direct-action day. They thought, I believe, that they were organizing along the lines of the Seattle model and they had a website, a defiant call to action, had set up a spokescouncil and made cool flyers and stickers. But they left out essential ingredients: a simple strategic framework or plan that would give a common logic and goal, and alliances with groups outside their political and cultural network. Given the anger at the Republicans and Bush, there were still thousands of people on the streets wanting to take some kind of a strong stand, but without any real framework, a repressive NYPD army simply rounded up groups at each gathering point as they tried to flee or avoid arrest. Nearly 2,000 of us were arrested throughout the day, but only a handful were arrested taking action on our own terms. Without a unifying action strategy with a logic to it, we were simply rounded up, defensively trying to escape the police.

Seattle's WTO direct action mobilization drew on strong networks and movements, including the student anti-sweatshop campaigns, Earth First! and forest organizing, anarchist organizing that had been growing and maturing during the years before, and some of the gutsier nonprofits like Rainforest Action Network, Global Exchange, and The Ruckus Society that stepped up and cosponsored a mass direct action. (It's worth noting that the Direct Action Network was formed entirely with grassroots local groups up and down the west coast of the US and Canada. We agreed to invite Global Exchange, Rainforest Action Network, and The Ruckus Society to become cosponsors in order to increase our numbers, capacity, and the range of networks involved.) Organized labor locally, regionally, and nationally; mainstream nonprofits like Public Citizen; and local grassroots groups put major time and resources into a massive education and organizing campaign in the nine months leading up to the WTO Ministerial.

Mass mobilizations around elite summits and meetings have been a key part of most successful movements, and serve two functions. First, they send shockwaves to demonstrate mass opposition and strength, to delegitimize, and sometimes to disrupt, and thus assert power that impacts the elites' attempts at globalization from above. Second, they strengthen and energize the networks and movements of our globalization from below. Strong summit mobilizations come out of ongoing campaigns, and are the culmination of movement-building in our communities. Six years after Seattle, at the Hong Kong WTO Ministerial, the Korean Struggle Mission—the alliance of Korean farmers, trade unionists, and others—who had come out of decades of militant mass movement organizing and a recent series of powerful, militant mass mobilizations in their own country—a December 1 general strike against the casualization of jobs, a militant farmers demonstration that left one farmer dead from police injuries, and a mass mobilization of 300,000 against the Asian-Pacific Economic Cooperation (APEC) Summit held in the port city of Busan. The point being that effective mass mobilizations and actions come out of strong movements and ongoing campaigns or struggles. They are not a substitute for them.

# Organizing and Strategy Lessons

## AFTER-ACTION ANALYSIS

After the Seattle WTO protests many of us went full steam into the next organizing (some took a break), creating a continental Direct Action Network (DAN), mobilizing for a joint labor-direct action mass action in support of the locked out Kaiser Aluminum Steelworkers Union members, etc. There were amazing reflections and accounts, but little analysis from a DAN organizer's view. (A couple of exceptions on the organizing/action structure are Starhawk's "How We Really Shut Down the WTO" and Viv Sharples' "A Model for Organizing Mass Nonviolent Direct Action" in the June–August *Peace News* from the UK.) We did not take the time out, and did not realize the importance of doing an after-action analysis of what worked, what did not, and why.

This lack of analysis may have contributed to a series of mass actions, still continuing, that do not benefit from the lessons that organizers—

hundreds of us organizers—could have provided. Radical researcher Paul de Armond's analysis of the 1999 week-long battle in Seattle, called "Black Flag Over Seattle," which appears in *Networks and Netwars* under the title "Netwar in the Emerald City," is still the best written. He writes:

> Law enforcement, government authorities, and even the American Civil Liberties Union have conducted instructive after-action analyses of the Battle of Seattle. By way of contrast, none of the protest organizations has rendered an after-action analysis of the strategies and tactics used in Seattle, even though the Internet teems with eyewitness accounts. In all forms of protracted conflict, early confrontations are seedbeds of doctrinal innovation—on all sides.

In a 2009 interview I asked him what lessons should activists have learned? He responded, in part:

> At the time, the obvious one was: How did this happen and where does it take us? At the time I wrote this, one obvious lesson to me seemed the unexpected political power of ad-hoc, even accidental, coalitions. Movements grow by expansion and recruitment. Instead, the movement [after Seattle] seemed to turn inwards to the point that some protests were an in-joke known only to the participants.

### The Seattle Model Takes on the Iraq War

In 2003, the United States invaded Iraq. Big oil corporations needed Iraq's nationalized oil and corporate globalizers wanted to force Iraq and the Middle East into the corporate globalized marketplace—at gunpoint, if necessary. The movement that was in the streets in Seattle—and across the planet—in '99 stepped up to try to prevent it. Global protests—the biggest in history—coordinated by the global justice networks that met at the World Social Forum, took place on all 7 continents, including Antarctica, and in more than 100 nations on February 15, 2003. In the San Francisco Bay Area, many of us who helped organize the Seattle protests planned to "create a social, economic and political cost" if the US invaded Iraq by shutting down

*Panicked WTO Delgates attempt to rush through the blockade only to find opening ceremonies cancelled for the day. Photo by Dang Ngo/ZUMA Press.*

*Photo by Dana Schuerholtz.*

the largest corporate and financial center in the Western United States, the San Francisco Financial District. Many of us had also worked to "localize" the global justice movement, linking local struggles with global ones. Seattle WTO protests were nine months in the planning and mobilized people from all over the US and Canada, with hundreds also joining us from around the world. We wondered if we could do it in a few months and with the local people in our area. On March 20, 2003, the morning after the US invaded Iraq, 20,000 Bay Area and regional residents brought San Francisco's Financial District streets to a standstill, and blockaded war-related corporations, government offices, and financial institutions. "They succeeded this morning—they shut the city down," said San Francisco cop Drew Cohen to the *San Francisco Chronicle*. "They are highly organized, but they are totally spontaneous. The protesters are always one step ahead of us," he added.

The sometimes-repeated notion that our success in Seattle was largely based on surprise is not true and ignores the lessons learned there. A month before the 2009 anti-G20 Mobilization in Pittsburgh, John Sellers, president of The Ruckus Society, was quoted in the *New York Times*: "With our success there [in Seattle around the WTO], we gave up the element of surprise, I don't think in our lifetime we'll have a large city police force be taken by surprise like that again." But the antiwar shutdown of San Francisco showed that at key moments, when we are well organized, strategic, and learn lessons, we can be amazingly effective.

One thing that happened in both Seattle, during the WTO, and in San Francisco, the day after the invasion of Iraq, is that an organized resistance catalyzed a broader public uprising; thousands who had no direct contact with the coordinating organizations heard about or witnessed the mass action, it made sense to them, and they joined in or supported.

## SEATTLE WTO SHUTDOWN STRATEGIC PRINCIPLES

Several years after the Seattle actions, a group of us called the People Powered Strategy Project reflected on the key elements that made the successful one-day mass urban action in Seattle. We came up with the following principles in an effort to bring a people-power strategy to the antiwar movement, which had none after the US invaded Iraq in 2003, and I have added a few more.

1) **Clear What-and-Why Logic:** A simple rationale for the mass action that makes sense to people. Direct Action Network wrote, "We are planning a large-scale, well-organized, high-visibility action to SHUT DOWN the World Trade Organization on Tuesday, November 30. The World Trade Organization has no right to make undemocratic, unaccountable, destructive decisions about our lives, our communities, and the earth. We will nonviolently and creatively block them from meeting."

2) **Broadly Publicized:** Lead-up actions, press conferences, a widely-distributed broadsheet newspaper, nearly 100,000 full color postcards, a massively visited Web site, widespread emailing of our call to action and action info, a West Coast performance/education/training road show and broad regional and North American mobilizing made sure many people knew what was planned, why, and how to prepare and plug-in.

3) **Mass Training and Mass Organization:** Thousands of people received nonviolent direct-action and related trainings in the days and weeks leading up to the action and in communities up and down the Western US, and well over a 1,000 people were directly involved in the organizing through affinity groups and clusters, working groups, and public meetings. The Direct Action Network was initiated by a network of local grassroots West Coast activists and was able to involve many varied segments of the movements— students groups, nonprofits, environmentalists, community organizers, labor organizers and members, and a wide range of activists and concerned folks.

4) **Decentralization:** A wide range of participating groups and individuals helped to shape, understood, and supported the basic strategy and agreements. At the core of the action were a number of self-reliant affinity groups who organized into clusters, thus the core action participants were well-organized, able to be flexible and make quick decisions, and respond easily to changes. This meant that the action was less vulnerable to repression or disruption, for example, if key organizers were arrested. Additionally, many like-minded groups and individuals who had no tangible or direct contact with our organization understood and supported the basic

strategy, and participated in the action without ever coming to an organizing meeting.

5) **Action Agreements:** The groups and activists of the Direct Action Network knew it would take a diversity of participants to shut down the WTO.

We made some basic agreements early on about what types of mass action would best shut down the WTO *and* would create a space that could involve a wide diversity of participants, because we would need hundreds or even thousands to shut down the WTO. We agreed that the direct action blockades would be nonviolent, and would not include property destruction (except for moving objects as blockades). We agreed that we would organize ourselves in affinity groups who would coordinate in a spokescouncil and that we would support and prepare for jail solidarity. Voluntary agreements are the foundation of any collective project and are the basis of trust for alliances of different people and organizations.

In the wake of Seattle, parts of the anarchist and anti-capitalist scene adopted and strongly promoted a "diversity of tactics" framework, which in practice means refusing to discuss which tactics are or are not strategic and refusing to make agreements about which tactics would or would not be used. It was seen as a pushback against the rigidity of "nonviolence" with all its baggage, allowing more space for property destruction and street fighting with—or fighting as self-defense against—cops.

Most movements around the world, nonviolent or not, discuss strategy, make agreements about which tactics are strategic, and organize to follow those agreements. Where diversity of tactics has replaced action agreements in the US, the effect has been that mass direct actions are less massive, less strategic, less frequent, with less public support, and more vulnerable to infiltration, repression, and corporate media distancing the public, and the alliance of groups and constituencies participating have become narrower.

6) **Open Organizing:** The decision had been made early on to organize openly, as mass nonviolent direct actions had been for many years. This

was a learned response to government efforts to infiltrate or disrupt past mass actions and movements, such as the FBI's COINTELPRO efforts to destroy the New Left, civil rights, and anti-Vietnam war movements. If a group's plans for mass actions or demonstrations are public and open, it is less vulnerable to government infiltrators or informants and its plans are not ruined if they are found out. It also makes group members less susceptible to the goal of government disruption, which is, in the words of one FBI Agent quoted by Brian Glick in his book *War at Home*, "to make activists think there is a cop behind every telephone pole." Our basic plan, to march on and blockade the WTO on the opening morning of their Ministerial, was very public, printed on tens of thousands of outreach postcards and broadsheets, and even on the front page of the *Seattle Times*. Keeping planning secret goes against the need to attract and involve large numbers of people, to have open democratic decision-making, which seems to be essential in getting large numbers of participants who are informed and empowered. Small self-reliant affinity groups of five to twenty-five people were the basic planning and decision-making bodies of the action, and did create an element of surprise. They formed into thirteen or so clusters to take on blockading the thirteen "pie slices," that downtown Seattle around the WTO had been divided into and some remained mobile. How each affinity group or cluster would blockade was an element of surprise, as groups were autonomous to do it as they chose.

7) **Media and Framing:** Direct Action Network aggressively communicated in plain language to participants, to movements, and to the public through our own printed materials, website, emails, road shows, and to both independent and corporate media what we were planning, why and what was wrong with the WTO.

This included:

✓ Distributing nearly 100,000 outreach postcards and 50,000 broadsheet newspapers with in-depth articles to potential participants and supporters.

✓ Numerous cosponsoring groups communicated with their own members, communities, and networks.

✓ Holding educational road shows; a People's Global Action caravan bus made stops in cities from New York City to Seattle across the entire country doing outreach events and media work as they went.

✓ Art and Revolution street theater troupe traveled from Central California to British Columbia giving popular education performances, direct action and theater trainings, and doing media about issues around the WTO, corporate globalization, and the global movements of resistance.

✓ Indymedia and hundreds of independent media journalists and outlets covered the events as they unfolded. Many participants also did their own media, writing accounts, taking photographs and video, sending them out through email networks, independent media outlets, and face-to-face report backs and storytelling.

✓ DAN held press conferences, sent out press releases, made spokespeople available, and aggressively engaged independent and corporate media in order to assert our views and perspectives before, during, and after the anti-WTO actions.

Because of this major effort to tell our story, and despite corporate media efforts to weaken public support for our direct actions, a month later, a January 2000 opinion poll by *Business Week* found that 52 percent of Americans sympathized with the protestors at the WTO in Seattle.

Too often, a healthy, radical critique of the corporate media leads to groups deciding to not even try to engage with them, standing by while they get beaten up in the mainstream press, and sometimes not even making the effort to communicate through independent media or directly through their own media and outreach. Yes the corporate media, like the police, are in part instruments of control, but would you stand by and not protect yourself against a cop's club, because their authority is illegitimate?

These principles worked for a strong well-organized mass action mobilization, with public support, to shut down one city for a day.

What would it take to do this in more than one city, for more than one day, and with increasing public support and participation?

## *Battle in Seattle*, The Movie

Now there is another story of Seattle WTO, the movie *Battle in Seattle*, created by Irish actor-director Stuart Townsend. It is a fictionalized story, with actual footage from the protests.

Townsend, the film's mastermind, began his career as a theater actor in Ireland, then became a well-known actor in movies like *Queen of the Damned*. He told me that he became bored with Hollywood movies and roles, and wanted to try his hand at writing and directing a movie about something that mattered.

He spent years researching, and pulled together the funding, producers, and actors, including his partner, actress Charlize Theron. The film was six years in the making, as Townsend explained to *NY Magazine*, "It took me a year and a half to research it, six months to write it, and then I spent half a year with a producer who then walked off the film. So I went back and rewrote, which took me a year and a half, and the day after I rewrote it I got financers, and after that it moved pretty quickly. And then we sold it to THINKfilm, and they imploded. So the film spent quite a bit of time on the shelf before Redwood Films decided to release it."

His hope was to see the film picked up by a major distributor and be seen by millions in theaters across the country and around the world. Townsend began making the film before Michael Moore made box office documentary hits like *Fahrenheit 9/11*; his plan was to re-tell the story of Seattle, and to get people to watch it more than they might a documentary by fictionalizing it into a pop movie format with requisite romance scenes, and fill it with popular actors and even hip hop performer Andre "3000" Benjamin. While the film was not seen as widely as hoped for, tens of millions of people did hear about the film through the many TV and media appearances by Townsend and the other film celebrities. It now lives on in DVD.

The movie follows several intertwined stories through the five days of the WTO—a European Doctors Without Borders participant, an

Battle in Seattle *theatrical poster.*

African trade minister, a TV news reporter and her camera man, a lower ranking riot cop (Woody Harrelson) and his pregnant wife (Charlize Theron) who works in a downtown clothing outlet, the mayor, and chief of police. But the four Direct Action Network organizers are at the heart of what everyone else is reacting to. It is the one story you can't take away.

When, in Fall 2006, I told friends and fellow organizers connected to the '99 WTO resistance in Seattle that I had talked with the guy making a mainstream movie about it, they urged me to find out what was up with it and do whatever was possible to make it better. The next couple of years were a strange journey of engaging with the movie and Stuart Townsend, and reflecting on, writing about, and organizing around the larger questions of 1999 Seattle WTO and movement history.

## NOV 2006: SLEEPLESS IN VANCOUVER

Though Townsend initially told me no, when I asked to read the script and offer feedback, I persisted in talking to him and his art department, and searched for a way that I might read it. I helped the *Battle in Seattle* art department, sending them a copy of the "pie chart" shutdown map and flyers. I talked to them about visual art, puppet and cardboard sign construction—which they ignored. I talked with Townsend about giving direct action trainings for the actors (which fellow organizer Han Shan and I did briefly for Michele Rodriguez and Martin Henderson). Townsend finally agreed to have me read and give feedback on his script if I came to Vancouver when filming began—ostensibly to give direct-action training to actors, and tips to the art department.

Michele, from the movie's production department, said she'd call me as soon as they knew what their film schedule was. A month later I got a call from Michele, "We start filming tomorrow if you want to come up." I realized that this was pretty much my one chance to impact the film, so I made calls and was able to get out of the next week's work and meetings. When she realized I was flying from San Francisco, not Seattle, she said they could not afford the ticket and insisted I pay for it when I arrived (which, after explaining I had just spent a week trying to help their 10 million dollar film, I did not). After agreeing to email me an official invitation that might have prevented the four-hour hassle with Canadian immigration due to past arts and nonviolent direct action trainings I had given in Windsor, Ontario in previous years, Michele later said they were too busy. After I gave Canadian Immigration Townsend's personal cell number and he put someone on the phone who seemed to calm them, they let me into the country (unlike the older South Asian gentleman trying to visit family, who they told was going to spend the night locked up in an airport holding cell while they looked into his case). I made it to a friend's house to get a couple hours of sleep before catching a bus to the movie set before dawn.

The streets were closed off and Vancouver police stood in the intersections. It was raining and still dark. I remembered stories from Canadian activists about the same Vancouver police who had drenched demonstrators in chemical weapon pepper spray and abducted organizers from the streets to squelch the global justice demonstrations at the APEC Summit (Asia Pacific Economic Cooperation, a group of corporate globalizers, including former Indonesian dictator Suharto) in Vancouver the year before Seattle, in 1998. These same cops were now rent-a-cops, hired to protect the recreation of a rebellion we were part of seven years before, the first of a series of strange ironies that week.

I found my way to Stuart Townsend, a pleasant thirty-something guy with a down vest, outdoor-winter clothes, and big boots, who was in the center of the beehive-like buzzing of the film production. He was friendly and hectic on his first day of shooting. I spent the day just watching as an army of skilled professionals worked around the clock to create the illusion of downtown Seattle during the WTO week and shot the first scenes—Vancouver street signs replaced with downtown Seattle ones; *Seattle Times* news stands were placed on corners; machines created rain when it was not raining; "tear gas" created by small machines, drifted across the sets. Anti-WTO protest posters with the color design from my arts organizing collective, Art and Revolution, were taped all over telephone poles and newspaper racks. Each day of filming, over 100 people were busy doing everything from camera and lighting to visual effects, hair, transportation, catering, accounting, etc.

*Actors playing Direct Action Network organizers on the* Battle in Seattle *film set; from left Jennifer Carpenter, André Benjamin (turtle costume with bullhorn), Martin Henderson, Michelle Rodriguez. Photo by Tamara Weikel.*

It was a contrast to the Direct Action Network in Seattle 1999, with nearly twenty-five functioning task groups and committees on the eve of the shutdown and over a thousand people self-organized into affinity groups, and affinity groups self-organized into clusters who took responsibility for shutting down one of thirteen area "pie slices" surrounding the WTO conference site. We were organized fairly horizontally, with many, many people taking on leadership roles and coordinating them.

Another difference was money. A few people had volunteered to be "extras" for crowd scenes in the film, but everyone else was getting paid. In DAN, we were all volunteer (though a few nonprofit organizations paid their organizers who helped out), and our budget a month before the shutdown was under $10,000. The re-make of the Battle in Seattle had raised ten million dollars—low for a mainstream feature film. I couldn't help but think that their budget could fund a hundred shutdowns.

Acting out a scene involving the takeover of a street intersection, fifty extras following directions moved uncertainly through the streets and took over an intersection, with lots of chanting and clenched fists in the air. It was a striking contrast to the groups of people in 1999 who were self-organized, experienced and/or trained moving with purpose. I suggested to Townsend that the people dressed as turtles would not chant "Turtles not Trade," but "Turtles not Free Trade," as most people did not oppose the exchange of goods, but did oppose corporate-driven "free" trade. Townsend directed people to change the chants.

A number of other Seattle WTO organizers somehow managed to converge and attempt to improve the film. Tachi, a Canadian activist living in Vancouver, took a job coordinating the extras and tried to recruit activists to volunteer. Shannon Service, who was a Radical Cheerleader and Direct Action Network organizer in Seattle, had come up to volunteer with the extras and do what she could to influence the film during the shooting. As the week continued, she would help to negotiate and implement some changes to the script. Rice, a student organizer in the Seattle WTO protests, was living in Vancouver and decided to volunteer as an extra, and ended up coordinating the other extras, leading chants, etc. Han Shan, who organized with the Ruckus Society during the WTO in Seattle, happened to be in Vancouver for other reasons, randomly met the film's production coordinator, Jim McKeown, at a bar, and also ended up intervening in the movie.

On my second day in Vancouver, I entered the film production office to read the script. I was handed the script, allowed to read it only in the office, and required to hand it back when I left. The first page read "BASED ON ACTUAL EVENTS." I spent the next three days sitting in the film production office back room reading, re-reading, taking notes, and trying to summarize the major stories and messages of the script. There was no way to really tell from talking to Townsend or watching individual scenes being filmed what the story was. My concern was less for historical accuracy than for how the stories and messages in the film would reflect the spirit and intention of the organizing and what people would take away from the film—would it make it harder or easier to organize for positive change?

Behind the front movie production office, a big room with five desks, was the art department. On one wall were dozens of low-resolution color printouts of images of Seattle WTO protest signs and art they had found on the web. I recognized most of the signs and puppets, which I, and many others, had helped create. The day before, I was saddened to see their version of our giant hand-painted cardboard ears of corn, which Art and Revolution originally made to commemorate the December 23, 1997 massacre of the Zapatista community, Las Abejas (the bees), of Acteal, Chiapas, Mexico. The movie's art department version was made of floppy real estate-sign-type corrugated plastic with kernels drawn in marker, and two stainless steel bolts attaching it to a stick. They had contracted a sculptor to recreate the giant cardboard puppet head and hands that I had worked on with Nadine Block and other activists, the arms of which were originally composed of Jan Berger's incredible mural-banner. The simple richness and beauty of some of the actual art is in the movie from clips of original footage—like Bread and Puppet's yellow woodcut insurrection flags—but the art department's expensive recreations were sad attempts at replicating our simple, cheap art of cardboard, used sheets, and house paint, images made by many hands with little money. It was kind of symbolic that the art department had no interest in hearing about the images and how they were made, and thus their recreation attempts lacked the heart and power of the originals.

On my fourth day in Vancouver I wrote to a handful of friends and fellow Seattle WTO organizers for help:

> *Ok—I've been in a florescent-lit movie production back room reading over the script for a lot of the last three days with people around me actually getting paid to create a simulation of the uprising we were a part of. It's weird. I have done my best to pull out what I think are the key stories and messages in the film script. Let me know what you think about the different narratives/issues/story elements and ideas for corrections/solutions/alternate narratives. I will write up the best analysis and solutions I can and get it to Townsend and other key folks as a first step. I hope to then engage in a dialogue and push them. I don't have huge expectations—they are on day five of filming and making changes may be hard. I hope we can impact the nature of the film and beyond that, the public's and movement's understanding of Seattle.*

> *Sleepless in…Vancouver, David*

I wrote up a summary of the main narratives of the film, emailed them around to a group of organizers for feedback and had phone conversations about it. I remember the silence on the phone from Anuradha Mittal, after I explained that there was no absolutely no mention or visuals of the Global South movements who had representatives all over Seattle during the WTO and who have and continue to lead the fight against WTO and corporate globalization. I then wrote up five major areas of concern, emailed them to Townsend, and set up a meeting to talk with him and his assistant, Greg, about them.

Here's a shortened version of the five areas of concern:

## 1) **PORTRAYAL OF ACTIVISTS**

Direct Action Network activists in the script do not reflect the values, culture and practices that were central to who we are, what we believe, how we work together, and why we won. None of the four DAN organizers come from community or justice movements—only from forest and animal liberation movements and their motives are not connected to how the WTO and corporate globalization hurt their communities and society. The organizers are shown in traditional leader roles, as opposed to the collective decentralized leadership that was practiced and key to success.

## 2) **GLOBAL SOUTH MOVEMENTS:**

Also missing from the WHY is any mention of Global South movements, who initiated and continue to lead global justice efforts, and any historical context. There were hundreds of activists in Seattle from grassroots movements on every continent. There was a People's March on N30 led by activists from the Philippines and joined by Global South movements and US people of color groups. DAN was part of People's Global Action (PGA), a Zapatista-initiated, Global South-led international network of radical movements. PGA did a bus tour across the US, and parked their bus at the Convergence Center and their international participants—indigenous Kuna Youth from Panama, Indian activists from the National Alliance of People's Movements, etc.— worked with DAN. Both the doctor and the delegate from Zimbabwe talk about conditions in Africa, but it is the movements, not the governments and western NGOs, that lead the fight against these conditions and their causes in Africa, Asia, and the Pacific Islands and in Latin America.

## 3) **PROTESTER VIOLENCE**

Throwing urine is a myth used by authorities to criminalize protest since Seattle and contributes to creating a climate of less civil rights and greater acceptance of violence against protest. [Some of the other concerning incidents of protester violence in the script were not included in the movie.]

## 4) **BLACK BLOC AND ANARCHISTS**

The group that broke corporate chain store windows was the black bloc, not "the anarchists." Anarchism is a philosophy and practice, which has widespread influence and diverse proponents. Black bloc is a militant street tactic (or those that use it), developed in Europe in the 1980s by "autonomists" and radicals—some identified as anarchist, many did not. The Seattle black bloc included people who identified as anarchists.

DAN was operating on anarchist principles, included hundreds of people who identified as anarchists and used traditional anarchist forms of organization (affinity groups, or *grupos de affinidad*, go back to the Iberian Anarchist Federation of Spain before and during the Spanish Civil War).

SOLUTION: Use black bloc, not anarchist, for the activists in black breaking windows. If "anarchist" is used, it should be clear that anarchism was widespread and included direct action activists in DAN.

If there is a black bloc vs. DAN conflict have it be over tactics and strategy: doing some economic or symbolic damage to corporate property vs. getting broad support needed for a militant mass direct action capable of shutting down the WTO, while winning public support and catalyzing a mass movement.

## 5) WHY WE WON

The script's implication is that we succeeded in shutting down the WTO because:

\* The City was caught by surprise by the numbers and tactics.

\* The Mayor was too lenient in allowing protest, and too slow to respond with chemical weapons, projectiles, arrests, and violence.

\* There were not enough police.

In actuality, our plans and indications of our numbers were very public, even if authorities did not utilize the information well. We won because we were strategic, well organized over six months, were part of strong local, regional, national, and international networks and alliances. We also won because leaderless networks are stronger and more flexible that the top-down hierarchies of the police, city, state, and federal authorities.

On their day off from filming, Sunday, I took a bus to the house Townsend had rented for his stay in Vancouver. I knew they did not really need me for anything and that they had already laid the foundation of the film. I also knew that this was the first time Townsend and Greg would have a real conversation about the movie with anyone from the Direct Action Network, whose story they were telling. There was too much to talk about in too little time and they were not in the mood to do much re-thinking or re-writing.

I told them that the real story of the epic global battle between corporate capitalism and social movements—in Seattle and across the planet—was a more intense story than *Star Wars* and *The Lord of the Rings* put together. They were open to specific changes in areas that did not require major shifts and had not been filmed yet, like reworking the scene where organizer Jay stands on a chair and, pulpit-like, tells everyone how they will shut down the World Trade Organization ministerial. I explained the difference between affinity groups (groups of five to twenty-five people that are the basic planning and support for mass actions) and clusters (groups of affinity groups), and how we made decisions in facilitated "spokescouncil" meetings with "spokes" delegated from each affinity group. They asked me to re-write that scene and anything else that I had problems with. I told them that I was discussing this with and would continue to work with some of my fellow organizers. I left the meeting with the distinct feeling that it was a little too late in the process and that they would need to feel some pressure and discomfort if they were to actually change anything in response to our criticisms.

## NOV/DEC 2006: GUERRILLA SCRIPT GROUP

Sitting around a big table in a flat with ten organizers who had been involved in organizing against the WTO in Seattle, Han, Shannon, and I reported what we knew about the film and our analysis of the script. I said that Townsend had agreed to consider our script revisions in the problem areas we had identified, although he was in filming and overwhelmed and I thought needed to feel some pressure to take it seriously. We decided to write a strongly-worded letter, to exert what pressure we could to get Stuart to make changes in the film. We also agreed to write up alternatives to the narratives that seemed to us to be most problematic.

Our letter read in part:

*Dear Stuart,*

*As some of the people who were deeply involved in the Direct Action Network (DAN) and in the demonstrations and movements portrayed in your film, we hope to help you portray events in a manner that is true to the intentions and spirit of Seattle, while telling a dramatic and meaningful story. We are writing to continue the current dialogue with greater clarity, and to formally communicate our concerns and requests. While we believe it was irresponsible that activists involved in the events you intend to depict weren't consulted many months ago, we are reaching out to you in good faith and with the intention of being solution-oriented. We will follow up this letter with specific and applicable script revision suggestions.*

*It is clear from the script and from the way in which activists on set have been received on set that everyone involved with the production of the film has the intention of portraying activists in a positive and responsible manner. However, we see many problematic portrayals of the Seattle events in the script and we are disappointed that dialogue with DAN participants and organizers is happening only now, more than a week into filming. This will obviously limit our ability to help you accurately reflect our motives, values, and practices. We are deeply concerned that unless some key changes are made, the film could unintentionally have a negative impact on global movements organizing for a more just and sustainable world.*

*Sincerely,*
*David Solnit, Shannon Service, Han Shan, Celia Alario, Antonia Juhasz, David Taylor, Patrick Reinsborough, Harold Linde, Omi Hodwitz*

It was strange to be working with some of the same folks I had worked with in Seattle, to plan a kind of a pressure campaign over the retelling of the uprising we had helped organize. Our group letter, together with letters from other groups who were helping the movie with old banners and flyers—Art and Revolution, Rainforest Action Network, and especially a strongly-worded one from The Ruckus Society—had the intended effect of making Townsend uncomfortable. People also talked to all the folks they knew who had a connection to the film or to Townsend and asked them to do what they could.

At our meeting we divided up the parts of the script that were most problematic to us, including the movie's postscript, and agreed to write the solutions.

I had written a summary and the key script sections. After I had done that, someone from the movie handed a copy of the script to another activist. This was helpful for re-writing the parts of the film we had problems with, but also confusing as we realized that the unofficially-donated copy that had just recently been passed off to us was an older version than the one I had been reading, which was being using for the movie.

Over the next days, people wrote new, improved versions of the problem parts of the script. The movie was being filmed as we were writing, so we worked fast. It was an amazingly talented group of experienced organizers, writers, and media strategy folks. Numerous versions and feedback circulated over our emails until we were done, with eighteen pages of alternate script that we believed would help solve the films problematic narratives. When it was finished we sent it with a note to Townsend and Greg, and we planned to keep pressure on them till we got a response.

A couple examples of our script solutions:

*Townsend's version:*
Jay asks Lou, "What do you believe in?" She replies, "When I was an animal activist I believed the strong preyed on the weak. When I was an anarchist I thought we could all be equal. Now I guess I don't believe in much of anything. I'm just getting a good long look at the enemy."

*Our solution:*
Jay asks Lou, "What do you believe in?" She replies, "Mostly us. The people we've been working with to make this shit go down. Our movement and the movements we're connected to. I don't know about you, but I come from radical stock. The Zapatistas are my guide. You know, the day they rose up and declared a national liberation movement in Mexico was the same day that NAFTA was signed? They've been fighting against this shit longer than my kid sister's been alive. And they've been winning."

Our script re-wrote Sam's identity from being a forest activist attorney to being an environmental justice organizer, who organized around the actual case of toxic MTBE chemical additives to gas (banned in California after a campaign, but the ban thrown out when the Canadian corporate MTBE manufacturer sued California under NAFTA).

*Our version:*
Jay explains where he came from: "Nobody thought it could be done. A bunch of activists—mostly poor and folks of color— forced California's Governor to ban the [MTBE gasoline additive]

toxins from gasoline that were seeping into their ground water. They kicked big oil's ass and you helped, Sam. And then what happened? 'Free Trade' rears its ugly head and the corporations get a new ace up their sleeve: NAFTA. The company manufacturing the shit uses NAFTA to launch a billion dollar lawsuit and the law you all struggled so hard to pass can be wiped away, just like that. Corporations trumping democracy! And right here, right now, the WTO wants to expand that NAFTA law around the world so even more corporations can use it to destroy even more laws."

Han continued to talk with Stuart, and I continued to talk with Stuart's assistant, Greg, and Shannon spent weeks on the set meeting with them and pushing them on small details. Shannon wrote to us after meeting with Greg about what they would change. She said, "Essentially, I agree that the five points are not fully addressed and I would love to see a more fundamental shift in the politics of this film. However, I still believe that they are a committed and passionate crew who are trying very hard to address them where they can. If we want our story done right, we'll need to do it ourselves. This isn't the film we would write. But, in my opinion, it's not an absolute travesty either."

There were some positive changes, but really it was too late to change basic narratives. Antonia Juhasz re-wrote the previously grim and inaccurate movie epilogue, which they used parts of. Shannon Wright suggested a montage using images of protest in the Global South, which they did at the end of the film.

The spokescouncil meeting was re-worked to be a little more like an actual group meeting and not just "Jay standing on a chair using it as an improvisational pulpit" and leading the meeting with call and response after returning from a banner hang to a hero's welcome.

On the negative side, even after being informed in-depth, Townsend repeated the commonly-used police disinformation myth of people throwing urine, which has never been documented at any global justice mobilization, but (much like the myth of Vietnam war protesters at airports spitting on returning war veterans) is used frequently by authorities to vilify social change movements. After I saw the preview screening, Townsend, knowing I had strongly objected to using this disinformation myth, explained to me that he had made it a resident, not an activist that threw the urine. It may have been a good movie device to make people sympathize with the cop before he beats up the protester, but it's also very destructive to repeat these myths.

A year later, before the first movie screening, I asked Townsend how it was to have us trying to intervene in the film. He said, "That was difficult. It was after shooting started and we had a twenty-nine-day shoot, which was pretty much… no one thought it could be done. It was great to have that sort of input. It was a little late unfortunately."

The spokescouncil scene with Jay was one we specifically talked about when I met with Townsend. I tried to explain the basics of our organizing process, and he asked me to just re-write it how I thought it should be. I told him I'd work with a group to re-write that and the other parts.

After the film was released, Townsend said, in an interview with *Cineaste*, "David Solnit ended up writing eighteen pages of script that he thought would be more of a realistic depiction of how a spokescouncil meeting happens. Unfortunately, it was eighteen pages of monologue, and I'm making a film, I'm not making a six-hour documentary."

He said something similar to me in person.

That interview, and comments he made to me in person, revealed that not only did he did not understand that our script solutions were by a group of us, but apparently he never even read them. How else could he think that all eighteen pages were about the spokescouncil scene we had discussed, instead of the reality, which was two?

Stuart Townsend likes to say the Seattle WTO was "the first Internet protest in history" (also a line in his movie); it's true that the Internet helped amazingly, but without the non-internet and face-to-face organizing, little would have happened in Seattle. What is true is that the *Battle in Seattle* may be the first Internet documentary (fictionalized, but still a documentary) in history. Townsend spent years on the Internet researching, but did not actually talk to anyone deeply involved in the story the movie tells. He told me, "In a weird way you're all like ghosts to me, like I've been living with all of you guys for four years and then suddenly… It was really kind of weird meeting people like yourselves… I don't know. You were a cast of characters in my head for so many years and suddenly you're like these real people."

I mentioned this to a friend, the award-winning Canadian documentary filmmaker Donna Read. She told me, "To not go directly to the people directly involved—the source of a story—goes against all the training and experience I have had making documentaries, your first step is talking to the people who were there and it's even more important to do this for a docudrama."

Writing a script without ever talking to the people whose story he tells is at the core of where the film suffers. The portrayal of organizers suffers, as he fills this information void with two-dimensional stereotypes of why people join movements, why they become active and rebel.

What is fascinating is that Townsend, a well-intentioned guy who has become quite sympathetic and passionate about the movements he portrays, actually repeats some myths and stereotypes about activism that are used by elites to damage or marginalize our movements. He was able to figure a lot of *what* happened through web research and reading, but when it came to explaining *why*—what made the activists tick, what motivated us, and how we operated—he relied on what he thought was his imagination, but may have actually been the mainstream myths and stereotypes about dissent and rebellion.

One of the difficulties in organizing for social change and public participation is that that mainstream media has waged a campaign of marginalization against "activism" and "protest." As a result, protest and activism are considered fringe and weird, instead of being understood as key parts of a democratic society, and at the core of most positive social and environmental gains over the centuries.

The four organizer characters in the movie are involved in forest issues and animal rights—one of them burned down an animal lab. Although animal rights/liberation and forest organizers have clearly articulated the connection, many people don't see these struggles as related to themselves or their communities. Jay, one of the Direct Action Network characters in the movie, has an axe to grind since his brother was killed in a forest protest, and Lou seems to have a personal issue with her father. The myth here is that people protest or rebel because they—not the system—have a problem. The activists, though intended to be humanized, are actually portrayed as "fringe" or non-mainstream, without jobs, families, homes, or lives beyond the protests, in contrast to the very mainstream cop with a family, home, and job, who is played powerfully by Woody Harrelson, the most three-dimensional and, I suspect for many movie viewers, the most sympathetic character.

The movie does explain many issues of the global justice movements. It also powerfully shows the violent police riots and repression that those in the streets experienced, but then lets the mayor, police chief, and governor, who were in charge, off the hook.

Townsend did not meaningfully engage with anyone in the Direct Action Network, who organized the WTO shutdown, he refused my offer of feedback on his script until after filming had begun, then he largely ignored numerous people who tried to help his film. Townsend did not talk to the folks whose story he told, so we talked to him. He largely dismissed the hundreds of volunteer hours spent by organizers to help his film—work that he should have initiated himself. Townsend and others making the film then claimed that they were consulting with me and other Seattle WTO organizers. I can't help but wonder, if he had actually talked to—and really listened and tried to understand—the people and politics of the Direct Action Network, would his movie have had more heart, avoided the common critiques of the "paper thin characters" he created out of his head, and been a more a powerful, and more successful movie?

## Celebrity: Opportunity or Danger?

Stuart Townsend was able to make his movie and circulate it because he is a celebrity and was able to access money, other celebrities, and media and public attention. In the US, social change organizations and movements often have little funding, and are largely shut out of mainstream media or are demonized by them. On the one hand, celebrities can bring media attention to a group or movement. The dangerous part comes when celebrities begin to decide, with their access to public attention and media, that they will just try to make changes themselves, without working through the groups and movements that are composed of, or in contact with, those who are directly impacted by changes or the lack thereof.

Activist and writer Stephen Duncombe explains our fascination with celebrity in his book *Dream: Progressive Politics in the Age of Spectacle*:

> Whether it's Angelina Jolie in Africa or Bono drawing attention to global poverty, progressives get giddy when a celebrity shares his or her spotlight with a liberal cause. This response runs deeper than rational appreciation for the media attention these causes are receiving; it's a sign of affirmation: left politics deigned legitimate by our modern gods.

> Understanding celebrity means looking beyond the stars themselves and questioning why we are so fascinated with them. One answer immediately comes to mind: they have what we don't and wish we did. Celebrities have money and beauty, but they also possess something far more important: recognition.

> In present-day politics citizens are barely noticed. We're recognized only, and briefly, as a vote or campaign contribution. From parties to advocacy groups, politics has increasingly become the business of professionals. People crave recognition—if they don't find it in their lives they'll find it vicariously through the stars.

Five years after Seattle WTO, celebrity rock stars Bob Geldof and Bono decided that they would use their celebrity access to media, money and power to solve African poverty around the 2005 annual meeting of the G8—the world richest countries meeting to decide how to run the world. Broad sectors of professional nonprofit social change organizations, charity groups, and mainstream grassroots movement folks, giddy over having celebrities join their cause, were co-opted under the broad-based Make Poverty History (MPH) campaign. Bono and Gledof became celebrity spokespeople for MPH and organized the massive global "Live 8" concert that overshadowed the mass mobilizations in Scotland as an army of rock stars and celebrities broadcast on corporate media on an unprecedented scale across the planet (Bill Gates was featured as a champion of anti-poverty efforts). Bono and Geldof had essentially cut a deal with British Prime Minister Tony Blair and Chancellor of the Exchequer Gordon Brown (who is now Prime Minister); Bono and Geldof would help portray Blair and the G8 as anti-poverty champions and, in return, Blair and the G8 would agree to some aid and debt relief for poor countries. At the New Labor Party convention, Bono labeled Blair and Brown the "Lennon and McCartney of poverty reduction." John Hilary, director of campaigns and policy at War on Want, was in the audience. "When Bono said that, to see the smiles on the faces of Gordon Brown and Tony Blair! This is exactly what they want—they want people to believe that this is their crusade, without actually changing their policy."

Not only did the G8 and Make Poverty History not talk about the poverty-creating war and occupation of Iraq, or poverty inside the rich countries, but they wrote African movements out of the discussion. Kofi Maluwi Klu, a leading Ghanian activist and international coordinator of Jubilee 2000 Africa Campaign in the late 1990s, responded, "We have a saying in the African liberation movement, 'nothing about us, without us.' Make Poverty History is a massive step backwards in this regard. The campaign is overwhelmingly led by Northern NGOs [Non-Government Organizations, as the United Nations calls nonprofit advocacy groups] and its basic message is about white millionaire pop stars saving Africa's helpless. The political movements still fighting for liberation on the ground are completely erased."

To the eventual dismay of many of the MPH members, Bono and Geldof had overshadowed, co-opted, and dealt a blow to much of the global justice movement in the UK. In exchange, they got the G8 countries to commit millions of dollars in aid to Africa. However, most of this aid was tied to "conditionalities" that required the receiving countries to agree to more of the policies that led to poverty in the first place. A few years later, little of the millions promised had even materialized.

Celebrities that have more access to money, power, and public attention than do movements involving millions of people can be dangerous and, if not accountable to those movements, they become deeply anti-democratic and actually disempower the movements and groups that need to be the engines of any democratic change. Duncombe suggests an alternative:

"By spotlighting the contributions of everyday citizens, we might, just might, be able to turn the public's attention away from celebrities and nudge it back to where it belongs: the people themselves."

### SEPT 2007: LOS ANGELES SCREENING AND INTERVIEW

On September 6, 2007, I drove to Beverly Hills, for a *Battle in Seattle* pre-release screening that Stuart Townsend was doing for a group of his friends, folks who worked on the movie, and a group of activists and organizers—most from nonprofit organizations he had come into contact with while making the film.

Before the screening I met Stuart at a local Italian restaurant to talk about the film. He was nervous about showing it, especially to me and the other activists. He genuinely cared what we thought and saw the movie as his form of activism, his contribution to the movement it portrayed. He said the film did not yet have a distributor and that would make it unlikely to come out in time for the 2007 Seattle shutdown anniversary, on November 30. He hoped to find a distributor when the film showed at the Toronto Film Festival. I told him I was going to write something about his film and my experience with it and asked if I could interview him for it.

Q: When did the Seattle WTO stick in your head?

Townsend: When I read Anita Roddick's *Take It Personally* book about globalization. And saw some images. It was the visuals that interested me first. I connected it with the event. I remembered the event vaguely and went on the Internet and started researching, instantly, I was like, my god this is a great story, just from what I immediately found. There is something about riot footage that really stirs me up. I don't know what it is. Maybe it was the Northern Ireland protests. Maybe I watched a lot of that stuff and it stuck in there as a child.

Q: How was your interest related to being Irish?

Townsend: Because we were the only white people that weren't colonizers, we were the colonized; I think a lot of Irish people definitely side with the little guy. 800 years of struggle, again, the same kind of thing as the riot footage, there's something about the injustices of the big guy against the little guy that really just makes me so angry. Makes me want to do something about it.

Q: Dissent and democratic forms of participation are marginalized in the film by portraying the participants as acting out personal issues or being a bit crazy.

Townsend: Tree huggers—the definitive term. One of the reasons I wanted to make the movie was because of that marginalization. I wanted to show how they do get marginalized. How the message did get lost, and the media does take spectacle over content and doesn't really report about all these nonviolent protesters and why they're there and about the WTO. It focuses on a rock being smashed through a window. I wanted the film to move a way from that stereotype, and show that these are passionate, dedicated people who've shut it down, and they do it by tactics that most people don't even know about. But the hard part was, you know, obviously, I'm not an activist... And that would have been where I could have used some help. Because they were the most difficult characters to write. They were really fucking difficult.

## THE MOVIE RELEASE

*Battle in Seattle* was released in five cities September 2008, and later showed in a few dozen cities for twelve weeks before going to DVD.

Leading up to the movie opening, groups of us came together and formed the Seattle WTO People's History Collective. We circulated an open letter titled "Will the Real Battle of Seattle Please Stand Up?" which read in part, "For the last two years, since before the *Battle in Seattle* was filmed, we have struggled with how we and the movements we are part of should relate to the movie. Some of us have also engaged with and struggled with the film's director Stuart Townsend and fought to intervene in and improve the film, with a small bit of success. Out of these discussions we have created the Seattle WTO People's History Project, an indymedia-style, participatory people's history website of our movement's own accounts, photos, videos, and reflections from the

Seattle WTO shutdown and resistance. Some global justice and anti-capitalist activists will intervene on the opening day of the movie to urge moviegoers to get the real story and make some history themselves." On opening night, activists passed out RealBattleinSeattle.org postcards, and talked to moviegoers in Seattle, San Francisco, Minneapolis, and Washington DC.

The movie ended up an independent release, without a large publicity budget, but one with a celebrity director and group of Hollywood celebrities making appearances at film screenings and in the media. Townsend spent more than a year before the release promoting it at film festivals around the world. He did his best to make up for the lack of a major distributor and a big publicity budget by making dozens of public appearances and media interviews with Charlize Theron and other actors from the movie. He also had a grassroots distribution and publicity strategy, getting unions and nonprofits to sponsor screenings, buy blocks of tickets, and publicize screenings. Townsend even hired anti-WTO organizer Harold Linde, who both hung the well-known WTO/Democracy banner in Seattle just before the WTO meeting and was part of our group of guerrilla scriptwriters who sought to positively impact the film. Harold made a website called "5 Actions," closely linked to the film, which aimed to get people who saw the film to take another step and do something in support of one of the five environmental and global justice campaigns he highlighted. The film also had a flashy website, with links to global justice-related nonprofits, background information, and also tried to use activist-style language as a marketing tool. You could even download ringtones for your cell phone of people chanting, "This is what democracy looks like."

Reviews of the movie were mixed. Much of corporate media criticized the film for openly sympathizing with social change movements and opposing the WTO. It received many positive reviews—especially from independent media—but also received many criticisms for having paper-thin characters or implausible plot gimmicks.

Many big, professional nonprofit organizations and unions were supportive of the movie, bought large numbers of tickets and helped to promote it. Rainforest Action Network had Townsend as the guest of honor at their annual fancy fundraising dinner. The national labor/

community group Jobs with Justice also had Townsend as a guest of honor at their annual conference dinner. I realized that one reason nonprofits and unions supported the film uncritically is because part of where it did fall short was in showing the non-hierarchical, directly-democratic politics and practice of the direct action movement—a politics and practice that nonprofits, their executive directors, and boards of directors and top-down unions do not share.

Rick Rowley of Big Noise Tactical Media, who, with Jill Frieberg, was one of the makers of the most widely viewed WTO documentary, *This is What Democracy Looks Like*, estimates that 250,000 people saw their film after it was released in 2000 and many people also bought and showed the video in the years after the Seattle WTO protests. He said of his film that, "it lives and dies with the movements," meaning that it got wide circulation because it was picked up, shown, and watched by a vibrant movement.

The bottom line for public film screenings is how many "butts in seats" a movie gets. The movie industry website *BoxOfficeMojo.com* says *Battle in Seattle* grossed $224,169 in the US and $662,292 outside the US. That indicates that it sold roughly 25,000 tickets in the US, which may be good for some independent films, but not for one that spent 10 million dollars. Many more will see the ÐVD version, which has been circulating widely. The DVD was released with special extras—interviews about the WTO with politicians and union leaders, the back-story on making of the movie, and a powerful short section where Townsend explains his motives for making the film and his deeply critical views on corporate globalization—an almost insurrectionary call for action and for economic alternatives.

# Towards A People's History

### THE US SOCIAL FORUM: CALL TO RECLAIM PEOPLE'S HISTORY

It was a still, sweaty-hot June night in Atlanta, and we were in the Democracy Tent at the first ever US Social Forum. Three of us who had organized with DAN—Jennifer Whitney, Brook Lehman, and me—decided to host a discussion about responses to the *Battle in Seattle* movie and the ongoing corporate media disinformation about Seattle.

About fifteen people participated, mostly people who were involved in Seattle WTO organizing or were inspired by it.

The World Social Forum has been held since 2000 as the global social movements alternative to the World Economic Forum (WEF), which meets every year in Davos, Switzerland. The WEF was a kind of an annual networking, discussion, and planning-how-to-run-the-world-schmooze-fest for the global elite—heads of corporations, wealthy governments, and a few notables and celebrities. The WTO was originally conceived at the WEF. The World Social Forum brought together people from all kinds of movements—grassroots organizations, professional nonprofits, intellectuals and academics, and many others. It was conceived as a space for movements to network and coordinate their efforts, and dialogue about alternatives to global corporate capitalism. It was held in Brazil for the first few years, then in India, Africa, and also regionally on different continents. The US Social Forum organizing was led by base-building organizations from communities of color and low-income communities, who had—in the wake of the Seattle WTO rebellion—organized themselves to assert leadership in the US global justice struggles. This Social Forum, in 2007, was the first held in the US, and 12,000 people came.

I summarized *Battle in Seattle* and how we'd tried to influence it. The groups discussed how best to respond. We agreed that it was important to remain independent from the movie, even though collaboration might get more exposure. We agreed to set up a website to facilitate this by hosting a people's history of the Seattle WTO resistance and resources for people to tell their story, hold events, etc. We decided to put out a "Call to Social Movements to Reclaim Our History," for movement organizations and participants to enter the public space and the discussion to tell and project our own stories when the film was released. We made copies and asked people at the social forum to sign on, which nearly a hundred people did that next day alone.

The call to action read, in part:

> It's time that we in the social movements tell our own stories, reclaim our own histories, and publicly fight damaging myths of our movements past and present. We must intervene in the

public understanding of what happened, what is happening, and what it all means. Stories are how we understand the world and thus shape the future—they are part of our fight against corporate power, empire, war, and social and environmental injustice and part of our fight for the alternatives that will make a better world.

The real story of Seattle 1999 is of tens of thousands of people rising up, taking direct action, and changing history; standing up to corporations and governments and winning; joining with movements around the world in our common struggle against the WTO.

Let's link the 1999 resistance to the WTO in Seattle and globally with building support for today's 2007 resistance that is continuing the fight for global justice on many fronts: against war and occupation for environmental and climate justice; for workers, immigrants, women, and farmers rights, etc. We call for commemorations, public events, performances, media, interventions, interruptions, educational events, performances, screenings, gatherings, and celebrations.

—From nearly a hundred participants the United Stated Social Forum, June 30, 2007

Perhaps the best way to challenge a false, damaging, or misleading story is ultimately to not just critique it, but to tell another, more powerful story. It is clear that what people believe happened in the past and the stories they believe determine what they believe in the present, and thus what role they may play in shaping a better future.

After battling corporate media lies for many years, and trying to intervene in the *Battle of Seattle* for over a year, I realized that what was really lacking was for people and organizations in the movements to tell our own story, to tell it compellingly, to amplify it. And I realized that how much we do this and how connected people in our movements and in society are to these histories and what they mean, determines what we think, what we will put up with, and whether we will rebel against injustice. Part of why it is so hard to organize in the

US, I think, is that there is much disconnection from and amnesia about our history. Radical historian Chris Carlsson says, "If people knew what we have been through and how things got this way they would never put up with it." I think of the Korean workers and farmers and their independent media movement, people who document their own history and activities with full color books, videos, and such, and commemorate their history of victories as well as the massacres and deaths.

### SEATTLE WTO PEOPLE'S HISTORY PROJECT

In Spring 2008, the Seattle International Film Festival opened up with a red carpet, star-studded kick-off event featuring *Battle in Seattle* and Stuart Townsend, Charlize Theron, and other cast members. The movie had been screening at film festivals around the world, but still would not be publicly released until September 2008.

Heather Day, a longtime Seattle global justice and community organizer, pushed the group of us who had committed to put together the People's History of Seattle WTO Project participatory website together in time for the screening. We did it, with the help of web designer Kate Khatib and web techie John Duda—both part of the independent media movement—and everyone's work on content. Seattle organizer Jeremy Simmer, who coordinated the University of Washington's WTO History Project, also worked with us. Local activists passed out postcards inviting people to check out and post to RealBattleInSeattle.org.

The postcards read, in part:

> In fall '08, a major motion picture, *Battle in Seattle*, will be seen across North America. It's a huge improvement over corporate media lies, but won't tell the motives or thinking of the people who shutdown the WTO. Only we can do that.

The postcards were made by the designer of DAN's original Seattle WTO postcards, Hugh D'Andrade, who had modified them for the occasion.

The website explained our vision and was an invitation:

Join us in learning, creating, and amplifying a People's History of the Battle of Seattle, told by the people, groups, and movements who participated and made it happen. It will only work if we participate and make it work. We seek to turn history upside down. We aim to replace their corporate media and elite "history from above" and their disinformation with our own people's "history from below." We are challenging ourselves, our diverse movements, and you to not merely criticize corporate media, but to proactively document and publicize our own history ourselves."

Jeremy Brecher, author of *History from Below*, writes, "Until recently, history was often regarded as solely a matter of what the powerful, the famous, and the wealthy thought and did. It was 'history from above.' What ordinary people felt and what they tried to accomplish was regarded as insignificant, not even worth regarding as part of history."

**PARTICIPATE**: tell your story,

**EDUCATE**: spread the word, and

**LIBERATE**: reclaim people's history so we can make history!

✌

*Photo by Dang Ngo/ZUMA Press.*

# THE MYTH OF SEATTLE VIOLENCE:

MY BATTLE WITH THE NEW YORK TIMES

By Rebecca Solnit

*"This is the west, sir. When the legend becomes fact, print the legend."—newspaper editor in the film* The Legend of Liberty Valance

## Making History and Making It Up

A few years ago I went to war with the *New York Times*, because they were lying on the top of the fold of the front page about recent history, lying flagrantly and damagingly about me and mine—though perhaps they believed their own lies. It was at the conclusion of the 2004 Republican National Convention in New York City, a festival of platitudes indoors and police repression outdoors. That season, various arms of the federal government were spreading suggestions that protesters were essentially terrorists and liable to be violent. Much of the media went along with it—Ted Koppel even flashed pictures of activists deemed "threats," during his program. The *New York Daily News* reported, "Fringe elements are hoping to spark major disruptions at the Republican National Convention with a series of sneaky tricks—including fooling bomb-sniffing dogs on trains bound for Penn Station, the *Daily News* has learned." In a long series of articles in the build up, during, and after the convention, the *New York Times* suggested that activists were quite prone to savage destruction, and used Seattle in 1999 as evidence.

Quite a lot of the things that everybody knows never happened. Feminists didn't actually burn bras. After years of searching for an actual incident, the sociologist Jerry Lembcke concluded that sixties antiwar activists did not spit in the faces of soldiers returning from Viet Nam.[1] These are two of the big myths of our time. There's a third, a new one, that is just as burdensome to the left: that the anti-WTO activists in Seattle in 1999 were violent. Many people believe that, and much encourages them to do so. Comparatively little has been made of the actual violence of the police in those days that changed the world, though there are no pictures of violent activists and quite a lot of Darth Vader-armored police pointing weapons at seated people, injured protestors, and more. The tale of activist violence is a background fact often referred to casually: the *Buenos Aires Herald* reported on the WTO ministerial in Hong Kong in December 2005, "But the fighting was less intense than that which marred the 1999 WTO conference in Seattle, which was the scene of huge and violent demonstrations against trade globalization."

Nobody argues that there was no property destruction in Seattle. The Eugene-based Black Bloc smashed a lot of plate glass windows in the central city area. Whether or not property destruction is violence is another thing altogether. Cutting down a tree to make a table—violent? Maybe not. Cutting down an old-growth forest—more violent? Cutting down the local regulations and rights that protect said forest as the WTO would have done—even more violent? Breaking a dish accidentally—not violent. Breaking the dinner dishes to intimidate your spouse—violence by proxy. Breaking the windows of destructive transnational corporations to make a point—kind of complicated, not necessarily endorsed in this essay. I saw the windows shortly after they were smashed and regretted that they would be cleaned up and repaired by workers rather than, say, Phil Knight, the CEO of Nike, though it must have been intimidating for the salespeople within, and I was glad no one was injured.

The police were another story. What happened in Seattle in 1999 was a huge, unanticipated, powerful—and rowdy—demonstration and blockade of the meeting of the World Trade Organization, met by escalating violence from police, who used tear gas, rubber bullets, truncheons, and direct assaults to attempt to take control of the city's public spaces. They injured many people. They eventually staged a nocturnal battle with the public on Capitol Hill, far from the site of the WTO and the downtown hotels, continuing their violence, and so outraging the locals that they fought back even though the battle was no longer about First Amendment access or the WTO, but about basic liberties in their own neighborhood. But the event was remembered as an occasion of activist violence.

Fairness and Accuracy in Reporting wrote, "CBS News anchor Dan Rather reported (12/1/99) that 'the meeting of the World Trade Organization was thrown into turmoil by violent demonstrations that went on into last night. That brought on today's crackdown.' A CNN report from Seattle (12/1/99) claimed that 'as tens of thousands marched through downtown Seattle, [a] small group of self-described anarchists smashed windows and vandalized stores. Police responded with rubber bullets and pepper gas.' But the sequence of events described in these reports was wrong. As Detective Randy Huserik, a spokesperson for the Seattle police, confirmed, pepper spray had first been used against protesters engaged in peaceful civil disobedience." Some mainstream media people were assaulted by the police; some reported on the police violence. The coverage at the time by the *San Francisco Chronicle* and the Seattle newspapers was quite accurate.

Official history is an accretion of acceptable versions. Before those arise there are great ruptures when the world actually changes and no one yet is in control of the meaning of what has happened or what kind of a future it will lead to—and perhaps these two things are the same thing. In these great pauses, much is possible, including a change of mind on a broad scale. September 11 was one such occasion, and in the days before the Bush Administration framed the act by a little-known group as the opening overture of a war, a remarkable contemplative stillness blanketed much of the country. The meaning was up for grabs, and even after the war on Afghanistan began, people continued buying quantities of books on Islam and the Middle East, talking among themselves, and thinking for themselves about foreign policy, violence, and civil society. That hijacking of meaning was doomed by its foundation in lies. Eight years later, most Americans no longer believe in "the war on terror" as meaningful, or the attempts to link Al Qaeda and the September 11 attacks to Iraq, and quite a lot of them believe, for better or worse, that the Bush Administration was complicit in the destruction of the World Trade Center towers.

## Maps of Change

November 30, 1999, a positive image to which 9/11 was the negative, was also one of those ruptures—the other half of the arrival of the millenium. No one, not even the organizers, anticipated that activists

*Photo by Dang Ngo/ZUMA Press.*

*Photo by Dang Ngo/ZUMA Press.*

*Used concussion grenade and rubber bullets.*
*Photo by Liz Highleyman (black-rose.com).*

would so successfully disrupt the WTO ministerial or that the success would become a huge story around the world, magnifying its impact. The event brought consciousness of corporate globalization and the arguments against it to much of the previously clueless global north. And it put the WTO on the defensive, encouraged the NGOs and poor nations to stand up for themselves, and helped transform history. Before Seattle, the WTO had seemed indestructible, its agenda of taking over the world and creating the most powerful monolithic institution in history inevitable. Four years after, when the WTO talks collapsed at Cancun, the organization was crippled, and it is now—as no one anticipated, though many dreamed—essentially disabled with no signs of possible recovery. What happened in Seattle mattered. "On the tear gas-shrouded streets of Seattle," reported the *Los Angeles Times*, "the unruly forces of democracy collided with the elite world of trade policy. And when the meeting ended in failure on Friday, the elitists had lost and the debate had changed forever." So had the world.

Some publications, including the UK *Guardian*, suggested it was the biggest political action since the 1960s. A foolish assertion, though I often think the real impact of the official "1960s"—that part late in the decade when young white people did some radical things, as opposed to the early 1960s when nonwhite people and middle-aged white ladies were the major force for change—was created by media enthusiasm. In 1969, 500 people demonstrating against something represented an insurgent nation to the contemporary media; 500 people doing the same in, say, 1989 were portrayed as anachronistic, naïve, irrelevant, and certainly not representative of anything larger. More commonly, even if they were 5,000 or 50,000, they were not portrayed at all. The media took a quarter-century break from American street activism. There were very large demonstrations in the 1980s and 1990s: the million people gathered in Central Park in 1982 for nuclear disarmament, for example. A decade later, 750,000 women, men, and children turned out for a NOW-organized march in Washington, DC On April 25, 1993, nearly a million people attended the March on Washington for Lesbian, Gay, and Bi Equal Rights and Liberation. The Million Man March was a largely African-American, overwhelmingly male gathering convened by Nation of Islam leader Louis Farrakhan in Washington, DC on October 16, 1995. March organizers estimated the crowd size at between 1.5 and 2 million people. Demonstrations against the 1991 Gulf War gathered even larger crowds, and mass civil disobedience at the Nevada Test Site reached a then-unprecedented scale. The '60s were, at best, a beginning.

In the 1980s, feminists, people of color, and antinuclear activists made great strides in remedying the white-guy-dominated charismatic-leadership style of much 1960's activism with attention to process, to consensus and other modes of dehierarchalizing organizing and communicating, to nonviolence action agreements, and trainings. (Of course people like civil-rights-movement organizer Ella Baker had already done this in the 1960s.) The idea of prefigurative politics—that your actions could embody your ideals and thereby realize them on some scale—became important. A much more sustainable, effective, unchaotic activism evolved from this. And the WTO demonstrations in Seattle may have been one of their finest flowers. The media woke up and noticed, for the first time in decades in this country, that nonviolent direct action in the streets could remake history.

None of the 600 arrests from those actions resulted in the successful prosecution of anyone for causing bodily harm (admittedly, a number of people pled out rather than return to Seattle to go to trial). No reports of police injured by protestors ever surfaced, and not because the Seattle city government was shy. The not particularly sympathetic *Seattle Post Intelligencer* reported the night of November 30, "In perhaps the single most violent act during a long day of protests, a small group of demonstrators dressed in black raced along downtown streets spray-painting businesses and breaking windows. They targeted businesses at random, from small jewelry stores to banks to fast-food restaurants. Most other demonstrators in the crowd yelled at them to stop." Of course that was not the most violent act of the day. Elsewhere in the story, "Even though police continued to fire tear gas or pepper spray through the evening, scattered violence persisted. About 15 minutes after the curfew went into effect, several people smashed their way into a Starbucks at 6th Avenue and Stewart Street and began destroying merchandise." And "One young woman who was in the area said, 'They shot us [with rubber bullets] and sprayed, but we're here protesting for peace.' She was crying and covered her mouth and eyes with a red bandana. At one point, several protesters threw a few plastic bottles toward police. But the rest of the crowd didn't like it and started

*Seattle, Nov 30, 1999.*
*Photo by Scott Engelhardt.*

*Photo by Dana Schuerholz.*

*Photo by Dang Ngo/ZUMA Press.*

shouting 'Non-violence!'" The tally for our side, or a controversial part of it: property damage. Their side: direct assaults on nonthreatening parties, including passersby and seated people doing nothing, often causing serious injury.

## Defining Violence

The 10,000 activists in the streets of downtown Seattle were only a small part of what happened on November 30, 1999. Seattle taxi drivers went on strike. The Longshore and Warehouse Union staged a strike that shut down about three-dozen ports from San Diego to northern Washington State. Sister demonstrations occurred across the United States and Canada. In Lisbon, Portugal, people marched, did street theater, and graffitied a McDonalds. In London, a street blockade was attacked by riot police, and people fought back with bottles and stones and overturned and ignited a police van. In Paris, 20,000 people marched, 800 miners clashed with police and ransacked a tax office and burned some cars. The demonstrations in Athens were lively too. In Geneva, saboteurs took out the power supply to the World Trade Organization's global headquarters, shutting down the organization's computers and communications for the morning. Actions involving less property damage and confrontation took place from Reykjavik, Winnipeg, and Limerick to Tel Aviv, Bangalore, New Delhi, Seoul, Melbourne, and Manila. The people had spoken. Mostly with bodies, signs, and theater, but with some rocks and flames too.

There are languages with extraordinary vocabularies for the phenomena they deal with: the Japanese have many nuanced words to describe types of rain; the Inuit have their many words for ice (not snow); Yiddish has dozens of words for annoying, incompetent, obnoxious and otherwise fallible people. English should have a nuanced vocabulary for violence, because there are so many kinds around us, including the kinds that don't get counted: the systemic and institutional violence the WTO sought to extend, the very violence activists from around the world came to protest. Farmers in France, Mexico, India, and Korea have been among the most audible voices saying that the WTO's rules and corporate globalization threatened their livelihood and with it a much larger rural culture and billions of human lives. To continue from the *Post-Intelligencer*: "But the movement to free trade around the world has become increasingly controversial as many tariffs are removed and countries increasingly challenge the non-tariff barriers to trade, such as labor laws and environmental regulations." Calling workers' rights and environmental protection a barrier says something about what the nature of that trade will be (and as someone recently pointed out, truly free trade would have required a one-sentence global agreement opening all borders and abolishing all rules, not the multi-thousand page documents that detailed what would be liberated and who enslaved by the transnational regulations).

# Hurling Incendiary Lies

Anthropologist David Graeber wrote that, three months after Seattle, "the *Boston Herald* reported that officers from Seattle had come to brief the local police on how to deal with 'Seattle tactics,' such as attacking police with 'chunks of concrete, BB guns, wrist rockets and large capacity squirt guns loaded with bleach and urine.' When, a few months later, *New York Times* reporter Nichole Christian, apparently relying on police sources in Detroit, claimed that Seattle demonstrators had 'hurled Molotov cocktails, rocks and excrement at delegates and police officers,' the *Times* had to run a retraction, admitting that Seattle authorities confirmed no objects had been thrown at human beings." Almost five years later, the myth of violent activists in Seattle had become common knowledge. On August 20, 2004, the *New York Times* declared, "Self-described anarchists were blamed for inciting the violence in Seattle at a 1999 meeting of the World Trade Organization in which 500 people were arrested and several businesses damaged." The nature and degree of that violence was not made clear.

After the RNC was over, the *Times* stated, "five years ago in Seattle, for example, there was widespread arson." Two days later, another front-page summary began, "Starbucks survived, the streets were not ablaze, and the police did not wipe acid from their faces or blood from their nightsticks. As the Republican National Convention departed, New York 2004 turned out not to be Seattle 1999, when window-smashing and marauding through the streets during a trade summit meeting gave rise to fears that any large political gathering would dissolve into lawlessness and anarchy." The implication was that all these things might have happened, and the overall coverage suggested that it was thanks to a massive crackdown on civil liberties that they did not.

I was furious, and though we all grow used to living in a world of lies, I decided that I was not going to let this one get by me. I wrote a letter to the editor:

> *The many recent* Times *pieces portraying us as, essentially, terrorists legitimizes police violence against us and helps to intimidate free speech and civic life. Traveling through Maine before I arrived in New York, I was saddened to encounter many principled people who believe that expressing one's political opinions in public is dangerous and frightening. In a democracy there should be no such fear. I was a participant in the Seattle demonstrations against the World Trade Organization in 1999... The significant violence in Seattle was police violence.*

Since I was furious, I concluded, sarcastically,

> *Perhaps the weapons of mass destruction the* Times *reported on so eagerly last year will really be found, but the acts of violence we are accused of in the past cannot, because they did not happen.*

That was a little jab at the Judith Miller scandal the paper was then involved in, the one in which a credulous reporter thrilled at her inside access became a tool for the Bush Administration to spread propaganda paving the way to war. She wrote the crucial stories suggesting that Iraq had weapons of mass destruction and posed a threat to the United States.

When the September 4 article appeared, I was even more furious and tried another letter:

> *Your newspaper seems deeply committed to creating a myth of violent activists. Twice since Thursday you have stated that the demonstration against the World Trade Organization in Seattle in 1999 was an event in which activists wrought mayhem. Thursday's front-page article declared outright "five years ago in Seattle, for example, there was widespread arson and window-smashing." I am*

*one of those activists, I was in Seattle in 1999, and I saw both the isolated incidents of kids breaking some windows and the incident that your reporter has transformed into "widespread arson." It consisted of one moderate-size, half-empty dumpster, well away from any building, on fire in the drizzle. Whether it caught fire from a misplaced cigarette, a police tear-gas canister (which activists sometimes throw away from the crowd as an act of self-defense), or an intentional act, it certainly did not constitute "widespread arson." Similarly, Saturday's article opens with events that only took place in the heated imagination of your reporters and the NYPD: "Starbucks survived, the streets were not ablaze, and the police did not wipe acid from their faces..." Was there credible evidence that such events were planned, or is this just a tactic to set readers' imaginations ablaze? The New York Times has been complicit in portraying activists, despite our widespread adherence to the nonviolent tradition of King and Gandhi, as essentially terrorists. Such portrayals legitimize police violence and repression of the legitimate exercise of first-amendment rights to free speech and free assembly. It is a blow against democracy and liberty of which the Times should be ashamed.*

When I calmed down, I realized the letters would never be published. The *Times* would permit disagreements and small corrections in their letters section, but nothing alleging that the very tenor of their front-page coverage was essentially propaganda based on lies about history. So I wrote to Daniel Okrent, the public editor.

*Your newspaper is eagerly slandering activists, in part by failing to investigate whether there is any basis to the claims of law enforcement that we may commit dangerous acts, in part by creating a fictitious history of violence at past actions.*

I supplied the quotes, my letters, and some background information. I got back an e-mail from an assistant saying:

*Dear Ms. Solnit,*

*Another reader raised a similar concern, which I noted to Mr. Okrent. I hope to have a response from him next week. If you haven't heard back by Wednesday please drop me a note.*

*Cheers,*
*Arthur*

And then on September 28th, 2004, Daniel Okrent himself wrote:

*Dear Ms. Solnit,*

*My apologies for this very late response. I was on vacation when you wrote, then utterly swamped when I returned.*

*I've done some research, and I'm satisfied that at least two of the phrases you mention—"widespread arson" and "streets ablaze" were inaccurate and inappropriate. I have asked the editors to publish a correction, and if they choose not to (although I have no reason to think they will), I will write about this myself.*

*Yours sincerely,*
*Daniel Okrent, Public Editor*

*N.B. All opinions expressed here, unless otherwise attributed, are solely my own.*

No one ever explained how you set streets ablaze; concrete is inflammable, cured asphalt is very difficult to set alight. I continued to press Okrent, and three weeks later, he responded:

*Dear Ms. Solnit,*

*On Friday afternoon, the news department concluded its inquiry into the original coverage of the Seattle demonstrations and the recent references to them. As a result, an Editors' Note will be published shortly, indicating that "widespread arson" and other descriptive terms were in error. Editors' Notes are considered far graver than simple corrections, and always compel the attention of the entire staff.*

*The Times institutionally, and I personally, owe you our gratitude for bringing this to my attention. As a result of your close reading, and your vigilant dedication to accuracy, the rewriting of this particular piece of history will be erased. Thank you.*

*Yours sincerely,*
*Daniel Okrent*

In early November, I wrote back:

*Dear Daniel Okrent,*

*Well, a few more weeks have passed without a correction, so I hope this does indeed mean that you will write something yourself as you promised on September 28. These slanders that were so widespread in August articles are a very, very serious matter, damaging the standing of activists in the public imagination, discouraging public participation, legitimizing the repression of the first amendment and civil liberties, and constructing a false history that justifies police violence and public fearfulness. As an activist and as a historian, I remain outraged. Many, many members of both these communities I belong to are also waiting for a correction.*

*Sincerely,*
*Rebecca Solnit*

And the reply came:

*Dear Ms. Solnit,*

*A correction appeared on Saturday, Oct. 30. Mr. Okrent said that while he recommended an editors' note, the correction editors decided not to go that far with it. But, it was corrected.*

*Mr. Okrent said he appreciated your careful reading.*
http://www.nytimes.com/2004/10/30/pageoneplus/corrections.html

*Sincerely,*
*Michael McElroy, Office of the Public Editor*
The New York Times

Here is the correction published that October 30, 2004:

> Because of an editing error, a front-page article on Sept. 2 about
> New York police tactics at the largely peaceful demonstrations
> during the Republican National Convention referred incorrectly to
> the violent demonstrations of December 1999 at the World Trade
> Organization meeting in Seattle, which the New York authorities
> cited as a cautionary lesson. Although numerous small fires were
> set in dumpsters in Seattle, there were no reports of widespread
> arson. The error was pointed out by protest organizations, and
> this correction was delayed for extensive checking.

The correction was as fabricated as the original articles. It characterizes
the demonstrations in Seattle as violent, situates them in December
(though the major day of action was November 30, 1999), turns me into
a protest organization (or perhaps an organization was also pressing
the *Times*), and claims that a major historical fiction was the result of
"an editing error"—and a single incident of such error, rather than a
repeated pattern of lies. How does an editing error result in a historical
fiction? Editors check and pare back writers' statements; good editors
don't pad them or add to them. Five untruths in three short sentences
is a lot. And while retracting the single charge of widespread arson,
the so-called correction perpetuates the myth of violence. Perhaps the
extensive checking was a search for evidence that they were right after
all, with the correction published only when they failed. (The *Times*
had published a similar claim about the Seattle WTO protests in 2001,
which activist protests outside their offices had forced them to retract.)
I regret now that I didn't continue pushing Okrent, but it sounded
as though he had been defeated too. Clearly the grudging and false
"correction" was not going to set the record straight. I did immediately
circulate my correspondence with Okrent and his aides to all my friends
(and had already taken up the issue in a piece for my online publisher,
Tomdispatch.com, that September, titled "Jailbirds I Have Loved, or
'No, You Can't Have My Rights, I'm Still Using Them'").

## The Nature of the Threat

What remains relevant is why the myth of activist violence persists.
My belief is that those who characterize us as violent correctly perceive

us as a threat. But to acknowledge us as a threat to the status quo is to acknowledge many dangerous things: that there is a status quo, rather than a natural order, that it is vulnerable, and that action in the streets can change it. Framed this way, activists are historical players who matter and whose danger may coexist with their legitimacy, even their heroism. To acknowledge this is also dangerous. Thus the threat has to be relocated from the legitimate arena of political and cultural change to the illegitimate realm of "lawlessness" and violence. Once this is done, activists are merely criminals, petty or otherwise, and their threat is part of the status quo. From the Boston Tea Party perpetrators to Civil Rights activists, the people who have made our world through direct action have been treated as dangerous, foolish, unrealistic, malcontented, unreasonable, and criminal in their time, even if they are revered when their radical acts are at a safe distance. The myth of activist violence is a way of concealing and dismissing real power. And maybe it's a measure of that power, if a frustrating, damaging one.

The graffiti on the wall in downtown Seattle that day said, "We are winning." We won the battle with the WTO, and though corporate globalization is a many-headed hydra, quite a few more of those heads have been chopped off, much of the world has been educated, huge swaths of it have been radicalized—no one, for example, foresaw Bolivia's future in 1999 or the death of the Free Trade Area of the Americas. And it turns out that ten thousand unarmed people in the streets can circumvent the juggernaut of the former most powerful institution in the world. Nonviolently. We have power. But we need to use that power to see that the truth is told and that history serves the truth, and justice. ❦

1.  See Jerry Lembcke, *The Spitting Image: Myth, Memory, and the Legacy of Vietnam*, whose jacket copy reads, "One of the most resilient images of the Vietnam era is that of the anti-war protester—often a woman—spitting on the uniformed veteran just off the plane. The lingering potency of this icon was evident during the Gulf War, when war supporters invoked it to discredit their opposition. In this startling book, Jerry Lembcke demonstrates that not a single incident of this sort has been convincingly documented. Rather, the anti-war Left saw in veterans a natural ally, and the relationship between anti-war forces and most veterans was defined by mutual support. Indeed one soldier wrote angrily to Vice President Spiro Agnew that the only Americans who seemed concerned about the soldier's welfare were the anti-war activists." Perhaps because of this myth, a Vietnam vet stood in line at a 2005 book signing by former anti-Vietnam-war activist Jane Fonda so that he could spit tobacco juice all over her sixty-something-year-old face.

*Street poster for November 30, 1999.*
*Image by Dana Schuerholz.*

# FIVE DAYS IN SEATTLE:

## A VIEW FROM THE GROUND

### By Chris Dixon

"Depends! Does anyone need some Depends?!" shouted the woman holding a plastic shopping bag. Hastily, a few people scrambled over to her. "They only cost a dollar," she explained while distributing the Depends brand adult diapers. Confronted with a few quizzical looks, she clarified, "You know, for lockdowns." Slowly, I understood: people who are locked together in blockades for hours at a time can't take time out for bathroom breaks. With diapers, that's not a problem.

It was the evening of Monday, November 29. Around us in a crowded warehouse, activists were making last-minute preparations, busily assembling first aid kits, painting puppets, holding small meetings, and welding odd-looking metal fixtures. We were in what was already well-known as "420" or "the Denny Space"—the official welcome and workshop center for those of us preparing to shut down the Seattle Ministerial meetings of the World Trade Organization (WTO), from November 30 to December 3. Formerly a dance club—complete with a bar, blackened ballroom, and industrial-size kitchen—the building at 420 East Denny Way near downtown Seattle was well-fitted to be a radical convergence space. And on November 20, with $1,000 in rent, a two-week lease, and some stark redecoration, it became a hatching ground for some of the largest and most effective protests in the recent history of the United States.

On that evening, as I sat at 420, the far-reaching success yet to come was difficult to foresee. For most folks across the US, the WTO was barely a blip on the evening news, another lost acronym in an alphabet soup of free trade agreements. Even for many people in Seattle, the WTO simply meant worse traffic and a larger police presence.

Who could have guessed the scale of what was about to happen?

Tom Hayden, '60s radical turned California State Senator, perhaps captured the fundamental shift best. Pausing in the midst of his strolls through throngs of protesters in downtown Seattle on November 30, he pointed out to a *Seattle Times* reporter: "Certainly the WTO, which was unknown in this country yesterday, is going to be a household word now—a bad one."

How did this come to pass? Indeed, how does one go about shutting down a major international trade meeting and launching a public debate about some of the very underpinnings of contemporary capitalism? When our culture is quick to remind us that the sixties are over, the left is dead, kids these days are jaded and cynical, and this thing called "globalization" is as natural and inevitable as gravity, where did the incredible success in Seattle come from? Answering these questions takes us on an intense journey, one that we can best understand from ground level—with a mix of tear gas, nightly meetings, and contagious exhilaration running through the streets.

A view from the ground means no safe pretense of "objectivity." Instead, it means looking out from amidst the police brutality, the marches, the graffiti, and the protesters. This is my view—that of one organizer, participant, and observer of what went down in Seattle in late November and early December 1999. In other words, this is a retrospective, an attempt to document and make sense out of what happened.

## The Road to Seattle

In late January of 1999, Seattle was announced as the choice for the WTO's "Millennium Round." By February, word was making its way through international activist circles. Many in the Pacific Northwest pointed to it as an unprecedented opportunity for protest, since the Seattle Ministerial was the first international trade meeting of its kind to be held in the US. Some of us had joined thousands of others in Vancouver, British Columbia, during November of 1997 to protest the Asian Pacific Economic Cooperation (APEC) summit as it sought to "open up" trade in the global Southeast. In Seattle, we saw the possibility of the APEC protests multiplied by one hundred.

By springtime, opponents and proponents alike were speaking about "the road to Seattle." In fact, the road to Seattle had many lanes and multiple routes. For corporate boosters like Pat Davis, president of the Washington Council on International Trade and one of the original supporters for bringing the WTO, it was about erecting the "Seattle Host Organization," raising funds from corporate sponsors, insuring the cooperation of public officials, and orchestrating a warm welcome. This road was fairly smooth—generously lubricated with both money and power.

For activists of all stripes, the road to Seattle was a far more difficult trek. Effective protests are rarely planned overnight; rather, they come out of patient, dedicated, and often-frustrating organizing efforts. Seattle was no different. Each activist organization faced an exhausting array of constant concerns, sharp debates, and endless planning sessions. How can we craft coalitions without watering down our politics? How can we get the word out about what we're organizing in Seattle? How can we effectively shut down the World Trade Organization? How can we make sure that our phones get answered? These questions and more plagued countless meetings, and without hundreds of thousands of dollars in corporate backing, underpaid, unpaid, and just plain tired activists had to rely on continuous grassroots educating, organizing, fundraising, and volunteer hours simply to stay afloat.

Even among progressive organizations there were different roads to Seattle. First and foremost, there was the People for Fair Trade/ Network Opposed to the WTO (PFFT), a group initiated in the spring of 1999. Launched with the assistance of Ralph Nader's organization, Public Citizen, PFFT drew together a broad umbrella of consumer advocacy groups, environmentalists, human rights activists, and many others. PFFT set the stage for much of what went down in the religious communities, on the college campuses, in the educational forums, and on the evening news of Seattle.

Another road to Seattle was articulated by the Labor Movement, which originally coined the phrase "protest of the century" to describe its anticipated demonstrations. Speaking of Labor with a capital "L" is a little inaccurate, though, because it wasn't entirely united—not in the months leading up to the WTO and not in the streets of Seattle. On

*The People's Global Action Caravan bus travels from New York to Seattle. Photo by Oakley Myers.*

*A pre-WTO neighborhood street festival procession takes off from the University of Washington. Photo by Oakley Myers.*

*Bread and Puppet's Jason Norris performs a street theater "cantastoria." Photo by Oakley Myers.*

one hand, the American Federation of Labor and other established unions wanted a foot in the door of the WTO. As Teamsters president James Hoffa put it, "We will have a place at the table of the WTO or we will shut it down." On the other hand, more radical unions like the Industrial Workers of the World, as well as some rank and file unionists, tied the WTO to larger, more systemic problems. For instance, steelworker John Goodman stated, "We all face the same problem and that is corporate greed." Regardless of some divisions, however, Labor easily mobilized the largest numbers that week, bringing some 30,000–40,000 people out to flood the streets on Tuesday, November 30.

Yet another road to Seattle was launched through a series of telephone conference calls and email collaborations among grassroots groups from LA to British Columbia beginning in June. Some of the activists involved in this long-distance coordination initiated a face-to-face meeting in Seattle in mid-July with people from several northwest cities. I was one among them. In August, these overlapping efforts merged and we decided to call ourselves the Direct Action Network Against Corporate Globalization (DAN). This group started out primarily as a loose conglomeration of peace activists, anarchists, environmentalists, international solidarity groups, and unaffiliated radicals all interested in street theater and/or direct action during the WTO. Many came from Art and Revolution collectives up and down the West Coast with enthusiasm for injecting brilliant art into radical politics.

The Direct Action Network eventually evolved into a more structured coalition, bringing together groups like the National Lawyers Guild, Rainforest Action Network, Animal Welfare Institute, and Mexico Solidarity Network, among others. The shared intent became, in the words of our call for mass action, "to physically and creatively shut down the WTO." That is, we weren't interested in drab, routine, and largely symbolic arrests to protest the World Trade Organization, and we didn't want to reform it or just "make our voices heard"; we wanted to nonviolently intervene, to stop the Ministerial meetings with art and living, breathing human bodies. As events unfolded in the streets during the WTO Ministerial, DAN came to wield some of the most clout.

At the international level, Peoples' Global Action (PGA) paved a complementary road to Seattle. Founded in 1998 at a Zapatista-initiated "Encuentro" with 400 representatives of grassroots movements from 71 countries (many of them in the global South), PGA developed as a worldwide network of mass movements resisting corporate globalization and the WTO. PGA also uncompromisingly called for "nonviolent civil disobedience" and "local alternatives by local people." And at its second annual conference in Banglore, India in August of 1999, PGA endorsed global actions in solidarity with the protests in Seattle on November 30.

In addition, PGA sent a group to—quite literally—travel the road to Seattle. The PGA caravan embarked from the East Coast in late October with a busload of activists from all over the world. Along the way to Seattle, they stopped in over twenty cities, "trying to communicate the impacts of globalization on our communities," as one participant, Sanjay Mangala Gopal of India, described it. Once in Seattle, the PGA caravan members were prepared to walk their talk. As Israeli activist Ronnie Arman, another participant, said: "We are going to risk arrest even though we know the severe consequences."

Each of the roads and routes to Seattle encountered unique strains and difficulties, but each converged in a similar spot. Indeed, that was a distinct part of the magic and power of what happened in the streets. Of course, on the way, there were some highlights.

## Escalating the Confrontation

On November 16, twenty-seven activists walked into the WTO headquarters in Geneva, Switzerland posing as students on a guided tour. With remarkable precision, several chained themselves across the front doorway while others dropped a banner from the roof. Meanwhile, one inside faxed a communiqué from an occupied office and another uploaded live digital video footage of the action in progress onto the web.

The Geneva action, which became ironically known as "Squat WTO," was intended to kick off resistance in Seattle and around the world. And it did. A few days later, DAN began a nine-day Direct Action and

*The Convergence at 420 Denny was the hub for hundreds every day; trainings, meetings, orientation, three meals a day, massive art and theater making, and lockbox distribution (the pile of tube shaped pipes used for locking to each other making blockades longer lasting). Photos by Oakley Myers.*

*Photo by Oakley Myers.*

*Photo by Dana Schuerholz.*

Street Theater Convergence out of the 420 space. The purpose of the Convergence was to train activists from across the globe for nonviolent direct action on the morning of November 30 (the day of Bill Clinton's planned welcome address to start the WTO Ministerial) and the subsequent time that many would spend in jail. The Convergence also provided a time and space for people to develop artwork of all kinds— from giant puppets of human heads to block-printed banners and signs to choreographed dance and theater pieces for the streets.

All in all, perhaps a couple thousand people participated in the Convergence at one time or another, a few coming from as far away as Taiwan and France. For many, the most important part was getting a grasp on the structure of the planned direct actions on November 30, and the legal strategy for those who were arrested.

The structure of actions on November 30 was based on "affinity groups" of five to fifteen people each, who would determine their own creative plans for physically blockading intersections around the Washington State Convention and Trade Center, where the WTO would be meeting. Each affinity group appointed a spokesperson who coordinated with others in nightly spokescouncil meetings and then reported back to their fellow members. Many affinity groups also agreed to work with each other in "clusters," which took responsibility for sets of intersections. Some clusters shouldered particularly ambitious projects. For instance, the cluster known as the "Flaming Dildos" volunteered to shut down the area next to the interstate highway running underneath the Convention Center.

The parallel legal strategy was based on the assumption that large numbers of activists would be arrested on the morning of November 30. With this expectation, DAN recommended that arrestees use "jail and court solidarity" tactics to get equal treatment and possibly get charges lowered or dropped for everyone. Chief among these tactics was arrestees refusing to give names when being processed. If need be, hundreds of jailed activists could also refuse to move or comply with other orders, clogging the legal system with their efforts. While people organized on the inside, the DAN legal team, coordinated by veteran activist and attorney Katya Komisaruk, would apply sustained legal pressure on the outside.

Besides nonviolent direct action and legal trainings, the Convergence also provided a space for funneling out-of-town activists into local resistance to the WTO, which was building in intensity. In fact, starting on November 21 with a colorful and festive neighborhood procession, Seattle saw almost daily protests and other visible actions. For example, the following day, November 22, corporate watchdog Global Exchange brought a few hundred protesters to the heart of downtown to demonstrate against the use of sweatshop labor by the Gap. Unexpectedly, as marchers reached Gap subsidiary Old Navy, two climbers rappelled off of the roof, unfurling a banner that read, "SWEATSHOPS: 'FREE TRADE' OR CORPORATE SLAVERY?" As the climbers and their support person were arrested by police, protesters engaged in conversations with passersby who turned out to be "generally supportive," according to Gray Air, one of many present. Throughout the week, Seattle residents would be largely sympathetic even if they did not participate in protests.

By November 27, two days before the WTO Ministerial, the tally of actions was mounting. In the middle of the night, activists had placed a fake front page on 25,000 issues of the *Seattle Post-Intelligencer*, satirizing its coverage of the WTO. A rally on the University of Washington campus marched the full length of a main avenue, occupying key intersections with guerrilla theater. A large squad of anti-corporate cheerleaders dressed in red mini-skirts crashed the annual Bon Marche parade through downtown Seattle. A critical mass bike ride, inflated to 400 anti-auto activists, rode down main streets, and eventually opened the doors of the Convention Center, riding straight through. Two courageous young women scaled a retaining wall next to Interstate 5 with a "SHUT DOWN THE WTO" banner, while one of their mothers shouted words of encouragement. Just by the looks of it, the WTO was in for a public relations nightmare.

Early on in the Convergence, Bay Area activist David Solnit had promised, "What you are going to see during the WTO is the largest use of street theater in history." In truth, we began to see this days before the actual Ministerial meetings began. On November 28, in the largest procession yet in the week, over 1,000 people paraded through Seattle's Capitol Hill neighborhood. Throughout, there were clowns, stilt walkers, giant puppets, marching bands, "radikal cheerleaders,"

*These photos taken by the climbers on the giant crane over downtown Seattle while hanging the banner. They were taken with a disposable camera and found years later. November 28, 1999. Photos by Erick Brownstein, Harold Linde, John Sellers, Shannon Wright/Rainforest Action Network.*

*Photo by Dang Ngo/ZUMA Press.*

and anarchist dance troupes. Even the steelworkers, who led the march, carried colorful, hand-painted pictures of snakes overlaid by the words "DON'T TRADE ON ME."

Later in the day, several hundred of us paraded into downtown for an impromptu protest at the Gap. Led by a white van equipped with loudspeakers, which blasted techno music and frequent interludes about the wages of Gap sweatshop workers in Saipan, we managed to occupy a major shopping area. Meanwhile, in the surrounding blocks, police on horseback prepared for riot control and an armored personnel carrier sped by. Although no major confrontations happened, the pieces for what would be an historic event were visibly in place: masses of exuberant protesters and a fully militarized police force.

## N29: A Beginning

Monday, November 29 was the unofficial beginning to the WTO Ministerial, although no actual meetings occurred. Instead, delegates began settling into town and the WTO invited "accredited" nongovernmental organizations (NGOs) for a day-long symposium. Later, the Seattle Host Organization treated WTO delegates to an opening reception and gala.

If the WTO was trying to be low-key, activists weren't. The night before, over seventy-five squatters occupied an abandoned building just one block from the downtown police station. As one squatter, Cat, explained, "This form of nonviolent direct action is not about just saying No! It is about saying Yes! and creating a real alternative. We are turning this into activist housing during the WTO and hope to keep it as housing for the homeless once we are gone." And indeed, they were able to hold the building until the end of the WTO.

Meanwhile, Seattle commuters started their work week in sight of 5 members of the Rainforest Action Network dangling from a 170-foot crane with an enormous banner that read "Democracy" and "WTO" with arrows pointing in opposite directions.

In the streets, 240 animal rights activists and environmentalists costumed themselves as sea turtles (protected under the US

Endangered Species Act—which the WTO has all but voided). Originally part of a Sierra Club march, they and nearly 2,000 others roamed downtown, eventually stopping to join French farmer José Bové in a protest at McDonalds. Bové, famous for bulldozing a McDonalds under construction in France, spoke about the importance of family farms in sight of two black-masked protesters climbing on top of a bus with a "VEGAN RESISTANCE" banner. Truly, the day was full of juxtapositions.

The solemn end came that evening with a "human chain to end Third World debt." Led by an interfaith coalition, nearly 5,000 people marched to encircle the site of the WTO's opening gala 7 times over. With chants and drumbeats, protesters persevered in the pouring rain, calling for the powerful member nations of the WTO to cancel the debt of the world's poorest countries.

## N30: "Shut It Down!"

Tuesday, November 30—known internationally as "N30"—was a day of competing images. On one hand, there was the power and diversity of countless people taking over the streets. On the other, there was the tear gas, rubber bullets, pepper spray, and brute force of the Seattle police. And somewhere in it all there were a few broken windows.

As I walked downtown with my affinity group at 6AM, actions were already underway. Workers were calling in sick, students weren't going to school, and some affinity groups were secretively setting up their blockades. Even cab drivers were engaged in a work stoppage. A week before, while discussing the WTO, Ingrid Chapman, a student activist at the University of Washington, had asserted: "This is *our* future." On Tuesday, she obviously wasn't the only one concerned about reclaiming the future from corporate globalization.

DAN had organized two public meeting locations on opposite sides of downtown at 7AM. On my way to one, I saw that police cars were present on every block. Suddenly, I stumbled into a flurry of flashing lights and watched as two women pushing a shopping cart with a puppet in it were surrounded by police officers. When asked, the police explained that the two would not identify themselves or admit that the shopping

*National Family Farm Coalition. Photo by Oakley Myers.*

*Vía Campesina. Photo by Oakley Myers.*

*Community Coalition for Environmental Justice.*
*Photo by Dana Schuerholz.*

*Indigenous Environmental Network. Photo by Dana Schuerholz.*

cart was theirs. After enough of a crowd grew to watch, though, the women were released—minus the shopping cart and the U-locks they were carrying with them.

Elsewhere, two other activists carrying pieces of a tripod, a large teepee-like structure for blocking roads, were detained by police and eventually arrested. Separately, both were interrogated, one pepper-sprayed and the other strapped to a chair and threatened with rape. Later, they were released with no charges. It was becoming strikingly apparent that the police weren't pulling any punches.

Protesters gathering at both meeting sites grew from the hundreds to the thousands by 7:30AM when they began lively processions toward downtown Seattle. In the drizzly early-morning dawn, there was more brilliant color in the crowds than in the entire drab cityscape that surrounded us. Looking around, there was a group of activist Santa Clauses; many returning sea turtles; a sprinkling of expert stilt-walkers; a jubilant squad of radikal cheerleaders; an indescribable number of puppets; an anarchist marching band, complete with matching pink gas masks; and hordes of regular-looking folks, ranging from steelworkers to yuppies.

As the processions neared police lines around the Convention Center, some affinity groups deployed blockades while others were already in progress. By the time marchers had circled the nearly twenty-block circumference, every single intersection, alleyway, and hotel entrance was blocked by nonviolent protesters. Some simply sat across roads with arms linked. Others locked their arms inside pieces of pipe known as "lockboxes," creating an impervious human wall. Still others used a combination of U-locks and bike cables to chain their necks together. One affinity group successfully set up a tripod with a protester sitting at the top and others locked to the base. By far, the most unique blockade, though, was created by a cluster that carried in a large wooden platform underpinned by metal pipes. Once set down in an intersection, activists locked their arms into each of the pipes and others sat in a circle around them.

Confronted with these immobile human blockades and thousands of their supporters, the police were visibly tense. Interestingly, Bill

Clinton had canceled his welcome address a few days before—perhaps anticipating its failure. The official opening of the WTO Ministerial was still scheduled for WTO delegates, yet, as mid-morning approached, they were unable to make it into the Convention Center. Some stopped to speak with protesters. Others simply tried to push their way through.

By 10AM, the police were preparing to create a corridor for "safe entry." They choose an intersection with a fairly simple blockade, gave a quick warning, lobbed in some tear gas canisters, and shot a volley of rubber bullets. The few protesters who remained were dragged away and arrested, many of them pepper-sprayed in the process. At a few other intersections, police resorted to more blunt force, beating nonviolent activists with two-foot long batons in order to motivate them to move.

Despite police efforts, the WTO was effectively shut down. Indeed, as Assistant Police Chief Ed Joiner would later flatly admit, "The police strategy failed." Word quickly made its way through the crowds that the morning session had been canceled and that the only people inside the Convention Center were the press. The following day, the *Seattle Times* would report that, throughout Tuesday morning, "US Secretary of State Madeleine Albright and US Trade Representative Charlene Barshefsky were holed up in the Westin Hotel. Federal law-enforcement officials said the streets of Seattle were too dangerous for them to travel the few blocks to the opening ceremonies."

Around 11AM, crowds of protesters swelled with the arrival of the People's Assembly march, made up of activists from the global South, and student walkout marches from nearby colleges and high schools. By that point, roughly 10,000 people from a variety of different marches and organizations had the Convention Center surrounded, and the energy of the crowd was high.

Although police continued to shoot cans of tear gas and steady streams of rubber bullets, most locked-down activists began to relax. We were obviously winning, with only a few arrests. Some people, like Portland labor organizer Nancy Haque, unlocked from their blockades to look at was happening in other areas around the Convention Center. When

I ran into her, she summarized the scene with a smile, saying: "We own the streets of Seattle."

Around us, some protesters had already begun decorating buildings with graffiti like "DESIRE ARMED," "THE KIDS ARE UPSET," and circle-A symbols. Others pushed dumpsters and newspaper boxes into intersections to reinforce existing blockades. This was an incongruous sight, for sure, combined with the shoppers still strolling in and out of nearby NikeTown.

While we were holding intersections, some 30,000–40,000 workers were gathering for a labor rally and march at Memorial Stadium, adjacent to downtown. As one organizer, Lucilene Whitesell, would later point out, this was "an unprecedented number." They weren't supporting strikers on a picket line; they were out on the streets showing international solidarity with workers everywhere. And by early afternoon, they were heading down Pine street, in sight of many of the blockades. Labor's unity dissolved in the face of confrontation, though. Some workers turned away by AFL-CIO crowd marshals marched on, while others rushed through the marshals to join the thousands already sitting or standing in the roads.

In the mid-afternoon, there was a brief and welcome respite. In a remarkable pause, the platform that activists had carried in for blockading purposes was turned into a stage. On it, members from the Emma Said Dance Collective (named after anarchist Emma Goldman who once said, "If I can't dance, I don't want to be part of your revolution") performed soothing body movements for hundreds who sat in the surrounding intersection. Slowly, a comforting tone filled the air as everyone began spontaneously humming and then singing "Amazing Grace." It was one of those once-in-a-lifetime transformative moments—over before anyone stopped to really notice.

As the day drew on, confrontation between police and protesters intensified once again. Those of us near major blockades became more and more used to the burning sensation of tear gas, and a few angry protesters began throwing the canisters back. Like many others, I was hit with rubber bullets while retreating from an intersection. A couple of blocks away, several young men set the contents of an overturned dumpster on fire after the police chased them down the street. Meanwhile, office workers and shoppers scrambled to get past the looming clouds of tear gas, many of them pausing to have their eyes flushed by DAN medics. Throughout, crowds frequently chanted "Nonviolence!" or displayed the two-fingered peace symbol.

Months before, DAN and affiliated organizations all agreed to a set of action agreements that prohibited "violence—physical or verbal" and "property destruction" for the duration of the Tuesday action. We collectively developed these in order to pull together large enough numbers to shut down the WTO and to maintain some level of public support. However, not everyone *in the streets* had agreed to abide by them. Since mid-morning, after police tear-gassing had begun, a group of black-clad and masked activists had been carefully busting windows at select corporate targets, including Nike, the Gap, and Bank of America. Using what they called "black bloc" formations, they stuck together and avoided police confrontations. As one black bloc collective later wrote in a communiqué, "When we smash a window, we aim to destroy the thin veneer of legitimacy that surrounds private property rights. At the same time, we exorcise that set of violent and destructive social relationships which has been imbued in almost everything around us."

It's important not to exaggerate. For the most part, property destruction was fairly localized. Many media reports described a city of Seattle completely devastated when, in reality, mainly corporate stores in the heart of downtown suffered damage. And in truth, only a few people actually engaged in substantial property damage.

Still, these actions sparked intense controversy in the following days. Labor leaders and other prominent organizers denounced those "rogue elements" who had "run amok," in the words of the *World Trade Observer*, a newspaper put out by a coalition of mainstream environmental and consumer groups. Protesters on the streets expressed their outrage as well. For example, Catherine Ahern was quoted by the *Seattle Times*: "I am so disappointed how this turned out. We had weeks of training how to do this peaceful.... Our message is not going to get out and I'm so mad." Others warned of the dangers of equating minor damage to buildings with countless acts of police brutality. The Independent Media Center's Lansing Scott wrote, "If we are going to condemn violence, let's be clear about who is doing what to whom, and keep things in perspective." Still other activists questioned the property destruction, not so much on philosophical grounds but tactically. Without any clear consensus, however, this was, and remains, a striking point of contention.

Back on the streets, the police were clearly agitated. As the afternoon turned into evening, rumor spread that Seattle Mayor Paul Schell had declared martial law. In fact, he had declared a "civil emergency" and set a curfew for 7PM to 7:30AM in the downtown area. "Many activists who were still locked down began to discuss leaving" as they saw that they could come back for another day of blockades on Wednesday.

Just as the largest blockade was calmly preparing to leave, though, the police opened fire with tear gas and rubber bullets. In addition, they added a new weapon: concussion grenades, small projectiles that hit the ground with a bright, booming explosion. In the face of this attack and pursuit by the police, scared protesters stampeded and splintered, many heading out of downtown. Several dozen fled toward the Independent Media Center, a small storefront resource for alternative journalists, only to be chased, sprayed with liquid tear gas, and then blockaded inside.

As many scrambled to get away from the tear gas and concussion grenades in other parts of downtown, the police hounded the remaining crowd of protesters into the nearby Capitol Hill neighborhood. There, residents and activists alike were tear-gassed and pepper-sprayed by police through several hours of repeated standoffs and assaults.

By the end of Tuesday, sixty-eight people were in jail, and many others had suffered the consequences of police repression. The DAN welcome center was turned into an emergency clinic for protesters with severe pepper spray burns and dangerous cases of tear gas inhalation. For all of it, though, we had successfully shut down the WTO. The *Seattle Times* quoted one of the last WTO delegates to leave on Tuesday afternoon: "That's one for the bad guys."

Presumably, we were the bad guys.

*Blockaders lock necks together. Photo by Dana Schuerholz.*

*Photo by Dana Schuerholz.*

# D1: Crackdown

Wednesday morning greeted Seattle with protesters marching into downtown once again, as the "civil emergency" curfew was supposedly lifted at 7:30AM. This time, however, they were quickly intercepted by riot police who commanded that they stop. While some held their ground and were arrested, others continued to march, outflanking police for over an hour as their numbers grew into the hundreds. Finally, as the march took a break in Westlake Park and welcomed more protestors, police surrounded the park. Police then separated people into those who wanted to be arrested and those who didn't. Then, all of them—"arrestables" and "non-arrestables" alike, including members of the DAN legal team—were arrested and dragged onto the scores of waiting buses. A crowd of hundreds loudly supported them from behind police lines.

NPR reported almost sardonically, "The police reclaimed the streets." A protester's sign was more blunt: "Welcome to 1984."

Under Seattle Mayor Paul Schell's orders, and with the help of some 400 National Guard troops, the police were actually occupying a sometimes 25-, sometimes 50-block area (depending on what you were doing and who you asked) of downtown with the Convention Center right in the middle. Entering that area without a "legitimate reason" (i.e., being a WTO delegate, law enforcement officer, resident, or office worker), became punishable by fines and jail time. In short, Schell had created a "protest-free zone." Civil libertarians angrily called it a "constitution-free zone."

At every opportunity, Schell enthusiastically reminded reporters and onlookers of his activist roots protesting the Vietnam War. And in the same breath, he declared it illegal to sell or be in possession of a gas mask, essentially signing a death sentence for asthmatic protesters.

The full weight of Schell's declarations wasn't fully apparent until later in the afternoon, however. As countless individual protesters were turned away from downtown by riot police, some 2,000 gathered outside of the protest-free zone for a short march and rally with the steelworkers. Most of us assumed that as long as we stayed with law-abiding union folks, we wouldn't be attacked by the police. And we still held onto that hope as we joined more militant trade unionists in a spontaneous march from the rally site toward downtown.

We were hardly a threatening bunch, mainly made up of older union activists, students, and even parents with their kids. Yet, over two blocks from the no protest zone, we were assaulted by a mob of police who tossed in multiple tear gas canisters and concussion grenades without warning. This wasn't the regular tear gas that we had grown used to the day before—we would later learn that the police had switched to "military-grade." The results were obvious. As the march scattered into several groups of a couple hundred people each, many older people collapsed. One man went into shock; a young woman passed out, landing on her face and fracturing her jaw in three places, after a canister exploded at her feet; and an older woman was hit in the face with a rubber bullet and temporarily blinded in one eye. The lines between protesters and downtown shoppers blurred as everyone tried to escape.

Still, the police relentlessly chased the scattered groups of protesters. At Seattle's famous Pike Place Market, some activists sat down to try to de-escalate the situation. Nearby, police reacted by pepper-spraying medics, shoppers, and marchers alike. One particularly panicky officer pointed a rubber bullet gun directly at a protester's head, less than five feet away.

As some activists sought medical attention, others simply fled. In the distance, more riot police amassed. A couple of hours later, these would be the police who chased a remaining splinter of nearly 300 protesters away from the protest-free zone, assuring them that they could continue their march if they went North—only to be fully corralled by "Peacekeepers," cynically-named armored police vehicles. According to one of the few witnesses who escaped, David Taylor, once the marchers were completely surrounded, the police threw in tear gas and commanded everyone to "get on the ground" or else face more tear gas. Then, over two-thirds were arrested—the remainder spared because the police ran out of buses to transport arrestees.

The following day, Kirk Murphy, a physician who treated many of the worst casualties of the day's events, described police actions candidly:

"What I have seen yesterday is the behavior consistent with someone who is insane."

And the insanity continued into the evening when, for the second night in a row, police pursued protesters into Capitol Hill. Helicopters with searchlights circled overhead while sirens screamed late into the night, punctuated by the regular sound of tear gas shots. This time, though, residents were even more furious at the military-like invasion, shouting at police to leave. A County Councilmember even came out to try to ease the confrontation. In the end, everyone—residents, protesters, idle onlookers, and even the Councilmember—were tear-gassed.

On the other side of town, at Sand Point Naval Base—which one jailed protester, Hank Tallman, would later characterize as "bondage summer camp"—seven busloads of arrested protesters refused to get off to be processed. Going for over thirteen hours without food, water, or bathroom facilities, they demanded to see their lawyers from the DAN legal team. By the middle of the night, they had all been dragged off, some pepper-sprayed.

Activist Jamie Ehrke would later tell how most arrestees remained undaunted, singing as they had learned in legal trainings, "I am going to remain silent/uh-huh, uh-huh, uh-huh/I want to see a lawyer/oh yeah, oh yeah, oh yeah." Throughout the following days, though, frustrated police and guards would ruthlessly terrorize jailed activists who tried to maintain solidarity. Just as one example among many, countless people were pepper-sprayed while in their cells when they refused to move. According to Tallman, some guards even used a technique known as "fire in the hole": pepper-spraying a protester in the face and then wrapping a blanket around the person's head.

What was happening inside and outside jails had merged. Weeks before, DAN organizer Stephanie Guilloud had perceptively warned, "Look at what happens to public space in Seattle" during the WTO. What was occupied democratically on Tuesday was aggressively retaken on Wednesday. The events of December 1 had shown that public space is always a site of struggle between ordinary people and state authorities. And because the authorities can deploy overwhelming force, they can often control public space.

Of course, the police called their actions "crowd control." But, as one protester, Brian Wehrle, clarified, "it's also class control." WTO delegates had complete freedom of movement while the rest of Seattle was barred from the heart of the city. Power was the ticket to mobility.

By the close of the day, the score was clear: if we had won ever-so-briefly on Tuesday, this was a very different story. The police had won on Wednesday, with injuries and mass arrests to demonstrate that fact. However, they had lost in the eyes of the media and, more importantly, the residents of Seattle. As I walked out of downtown that evening, people were gathered in bars and cafés watching live footage on TV of riot police firing tear gas and rubber bullets into protesters. Standing outside of one storefront, I overheard some downtown office workers talking about the "craziness" of Schell's declarations. Meanwhile, many shopkeepers had put up signs in their windows, like "WTO, GO HOME" or "We support peaceful protesters."

# D2: This Is What Democracy Looks Like!

Thursday, December 2, was notably lighter than previous days. Perhaps the sun shining had something to do with it, or perhaps it was because the police, obviously concerned about their image and public opinion, kept a lower profile.

Activists continued to persevere. Starting from Capitol Hill, over 2,000 people marched toward downtown. It was, by far, the most colorful procession since Tuesday morning. Indeed, it was more like a parade than a protest. Marchers carried signs, flags, banners, towering skeleton puppets, and a giant human head flanked by two large hands connected with painted banner-sleeves. Like many of the protesters, the human head was gagged in order to visually communicate the effects of Mayor Schell's declarations. Offering further comment, one marcher's sign read: "THIS IS A FREE PROTEST ZONE."

As I caught up with the march, a song wafted through the crowd: "We have come too far/We won't turn around/We'll flood the streets with justice/We are freedom bound." In counterpoint, others chanted, "This is what democracy looks like!" Together, the song and chant provided an aural backdrop that reinforced our collective sense of power.

*Neigbors confront Seattle Police on Capital Hill.*
*Photo by Dana Schuerholz.*

*"State of Emergency" is declared by officals, a downtown Seattle*
*curfew set and the Washington National Guard's 81st Infantry*
*Brigade, 1-303 Armor Battalion, and the 898th Combat Engineer*
*Battalion deployed. Photos by Dang Ngo/ZUMA Press.*

Along the way, motorcycle police directed traffic as we flashed peace signs at them. At one intersection, a protester pointedly asked, "This is way more fun, isn't it?" Almost unconsciously, one of the officers responded, "Uh-huh."

Of course, the riot police were still there—just not so visibly. As our march joined a rally led by small farmers next to Pike Place Market, someone mentioned that police vans full of ready and waiting armored officers were just up around the block, out of sight but not out of mind.

Following the rally, marchers split into two processions—one heading to protest at multinational agribusiness company Cargill and another aiming toward major WTO sponsor and timber corporation Weyerhaeuser. The vast majority—upwards of 2,000—followed the latter, briefly stopping at Weyerhaeuser's Seattle headquarters to hang banners and shout some chants, and then moving to the county jail, where many of the nearly 500 arrested protesters were being held.

As we arrived, riot police blocked off the nearby freeway entrance, fearing that we would occupy the interstate. Our focus, however, was on the people inside. Someone held a hand-written cardboard sign: "FREE THE SEATTLE 500, JAIL THE FORTUNE 500." Marching around, we could see prisoners pressed up against cell windows and raising fists. Hank Tallman, in jail at the time, later said that, in his one phone call, the DAN legal team had mentioned the 2,000 outside. "I turned to the rest of the prisoners in the cell block and yelled," he said. "They were all cheering." Outside, we began to hold hands to encircle the building. Others gathered near the front and we soon heard that an affinity group had physically blockaded the main entrance. Tension was mounting, with many of us preparing for tear gas, but the police maintained only a light presence.

Within an hour, the blockading affinity group announced their demands: unconditional freedom for all nonviolent protesters and a public apology from the city of Seattle. Those of us who were willing to risk arrest began joining the others at the entrance, overflowing into the sidewalk and onto the street. Still, the police stuck to the periphery. We appeared to be in a protracted standoff, and patiently we waited.

As the sun set, a representative from the DAN legal team announced that they had been negotiating with city officials who had granted a concession: if we ended the blockade, they would allow pairs of DAN lawyers and paralegals (in other words, organizers) to consult with groups of jailed protesters. Many present grumbled, saying that the city was only allowing prisoners the rights already owed to them. The affinity group that had sparked the action, however, urged us to exit the blockade with them. And slowly but surely, protesters began to march home.

Earlier in the day, Texas populist and humorist Jim Hightower had characterized the week of WTO protests as an "unscheduled outbreak of democracy." From beginning to end, that's exactly what Thursday was about. After day-long public criticism of the police actions on Capitol Hill, Mayor Schell had dropped his enforced curfew and trimmed his no protest zone. Meanwhile, activists outside the county jail had successfully pressured reluctant public officials into negotiations. We were getting a taste of real democracy motivated, as it always is, by popular collective action.

# D3: Success

By Friday, most WTO protesters were dragging. After a week of running from riot police, inhaling tear gas, and enduring constant sleep deprivation, many were looking for a sense of closure, as well as more news about the 500 still in jail.

As a final mass action for the week, the County Labor Council organized a rally and march from the local labor temple. Altogether, several thousand people wound their way through downtown with shouts of encouragement from construction workers, motorists, and other passersby.

At the conclusion of the march, a large group of protesters—now including many Seattle residents who were simply pissed off at Mayor Schell's declarations—turned back toward downtown. As the spontaneous march approached police lines, minor confrontations erupted, and protesters argued about whether we should focus on the WTO or those who were in jail. In the end, there was no resolution,

*WTO delgate prevented from reaching the Ministerial.*
*Photo by Dang Ngo/ZUMA Press.*

*People, puppets, and a tripod blockade (behind puppet with flag) surround the*
*WTO. Nov 30, 1999. Photo by Dana Schuerholz.*

with the march breaking in half: one group went to the jail and another remained in sight of the Convention Center.

Once at the jail, several hundred gathered to try to sort out what we could do for those still inside. To chants of "let them go!", DAN legal team coordinator Katya Komisaruk reported that many arrested protesters were being brutalized and separated from each other. In addition, some weren't getting the food and medical treatment that they needed.

From there, the rest of the day was an exercise in direct democracy as protester Skip Spitzer volunteered to facilitate a meeting of the hundreds present. Twenty-three people presented proposals for how best to force the city to negotiate with our legal team, and then we promptly split into smaller groups to discuss them. Each group reached a consensus on what it favored and then sent a spokesperson to hammer it out with some twenty other spokespeople. Within two hours, we had an action plan to occupy the main entrance of the jail until all the protesters were released; to invite the rest of Seattle to join us; to demand that the Mayor, County Executive, and City Attorney negotiate with us; and to insist on proper medical care and food for those inside the jail. From there, we began making preparations for a long stay into the bone-chilling night.

While we were making our decisions at the jail, the other half of our march had chosen to blockade the Westin Hotel, where many WTO delegates were staying. An affinity group of eight people U-locked themselves to the main entrances while hundreds of others occupied the road and sidewalk in front. Police kept their distance, however.

As both groups hunkered down, news leaked from the Convention Center that the WTO Ministerial had ended—with no agreement on a new round of meetings. Earlier that morning, the African delegation had booed the US Trade Representative as she walked into a plenary session. And as the day came to a close, a coalition of delegates from over seventy countries in Africa, Latin America, and Asia had stubbornly refused to sign onto an agenda in which they saw they had little voice. Of course, the WTO wasn't dead, but it was severely stalled. The next day, the *Seattle Post-Intelligencer*'s bold headline put it tersely:

"Summit ends in failure." Our efforts had contributed, some delegates would later admit, by costing the Ministerial nearly two full days of meeting time.

With the word of success, occupations at the jail and the Westin turned into street parties with dancing, drumming, and singing into the late hours of the night. Reportedly, even police danced a few steps. At the hotel, protesters also used the opportunity to sing "Happy Birthday" to one among them, and then to a police officer, who admitted it was his birthday, too.

The commitment of protesters was only buoyed by the news. At least 100 stayed in each location through the night. Those at the Westin finally decided to unlock the next morning, reasoning that, if arrested, their message wouldn't be clear and that they had already achieved most of their goals. In contrast, the occupation of the jail would continue for days, until most of the arrested protesters were released on Sunday, December 5.

On Thursday, we had learned the chant, "WTO, you've gotta go/The people came and stole the show." It was no more apt than on that Friday night as WTO delegates prepared to leave town. As many commentators would later point out, thousands of us went up against one of the most powerful organizations in the world. And we won.

## Postscript: What If We Could Win?

I wrote this account for *Punk Planet* magazine in the week immediately following the Seattle WTO protests. I was still recovering from tear gas inhalation, my ears were still ringing with the blasts of concussion grenades, and I was anxiously waiting for some friends to get out of jail. And yet, despite all of that, I was propelled by a sense of hope and possibility that I had never experienced in my previous seven years as an activist.

At the time, all of us who had organized for the Seattle actions were trying to assess what we had done and what it all meant. In the years since, however, an unfortunate and distorted mythology has developed around the Seattle protests.

There are two kinds of myths that I think are especially counterproductive. The first is that what we did was somehow altogether new. In fact, our efforts in Seattle closely followed in the footsteps of militant movements in the global South, which have led the global revolt against neoliberalism. This started with protests against structural adjustment measures in the 1980s and came together even more coherently with the emergence of the Zapatistas in the 1990s. In addition, our strategies and tactics in Seattle—from affinity groups to direct action—importantly grew out of the histories and experiences of previous US-based movements, including labor radicalism associated with the Industrial Workers of the World, revolutionary pacifist efforts, grassroots initiatives in the Civil Rights Movement like the Student Nonviolent Coordinating Committee, various strands of feminist organizing, and the queer radicalism of groups like ACT UP. And finally, if we understand neoliberalism as a continuation of colonization and capitalism, our rebellion in Seattle was connected to a history of Indigenous resistance that is over 500 years old.

In 2001, La Convergence des luttes anti-capitalistes/the Anti-Capitalist Convergence in Montréal was busily preparing for protests at the Summit of the Americas in Québec City. They coined the slogan: "It didn't start in Seattle...and it sure as hell isn't going to stop with Québec." We would do well to remember this, and to appreciate and explore histories and continuities across our movements.

The second kind of counterproductive myth is that what we did in Seattle was heroic and flawless. The reality is that we made many mistakes. As DAN organizer Stephanie Guilloud would later write, "We were not building a long-term resistance movement: we were mobilizing for a protest." And while we were caught up in the excitement and urgency of mobilizing, it was easy to overlook the fact that we were predominantly white and middle-class. Indeed, our privileges framed our experiences in many ways. For one, few of us considered what it would mean to organize beyond the constituencies with whom we were most comfortable—largely anarchists, direct action environmentalists, and international solidarity activists. As well, many of us didn't think about the different meanings and risks of direct action tactics among communities that are faced with police repression every day. And many of us were only beginning to think about the interconnections between global capitalism, hetero-patriarchy, racism, and other systems of domination.

As we focused on mobilizing for the WTO protests, we also didn't think carefully enough about laying the foundations for a resilient movement grounded in diverse communities. Many of us were satisfied to stay within our limited activist networks and comfortable social scenes. As a result, we weren't pushing ourselves to grapple with pressing questions: In what ways should we be consciously connecting our efforts to community-based struggles for justice and dignity? And how, concretely, should we be contributing to building long-term and large-scale movements? These questions continue to be some of the most important ones for us to address in our work.

Challenging the mythology doesn't mean letting go of what we accomplished in Seattle. I still keep a photo on my wall of the graffiti that was chalked and spray-painted all over downtown Seattle on November 30: "WE ARE WINNING—DON'T FORGET." By that point, this was hardly an exaggeration. Yet, twenty-four hours earlier, as activists were passing out Depends and making final preparations, very few were considering what it would mean to actually succeed. Like many, I assumed that the police would clear out the blockades with mass arrests on Tuesday morning and we would spend the rest of the week trying to get protesters out of jail. Instead, we did what we thought was impossible—we shut down the WTO.

Our resounding victory is the most enduring legacy of the Seattle protests. Through direct action and direct democracy, thousands of ordinary people—workers, parents, community organizers, students, activists, and many others—made history. We contributed to fundamentally shifting public discussions about globalization, economic inequality, and environmental devastation. Meanwhile, we unequivocally communicated to people across the globe that there are many in the US who refuse neoliberalism and are working to develop other worlds ruled not by profit but by values of democracy, cooperation, equality, and sustainability.

What we did in Seattle in 1999 wasn't perfect. Movements never are. But it was an amazing victory, one that can and should still inspire us. We need to consciously celebrate it and soberly learn from it. ✌

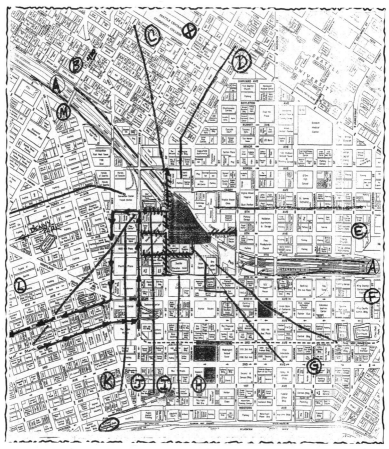

*Original Direct Action Network WTO blockade map dividing downtown
Seattle into thirteen "pie slices" surrounding the WTO Ministerial held
at the Washington Convention & Trade Center (dark triangle in center).
Section "A" is Interstate Hwy 5, which cuts through downtown Seattle and
directly under part of the WTO/Convention Center. Different clusters of
affinity groups took responsibility for blocking each pie-slice section. Two
7AM marches descended on the WTO Meeting site from both sides, one
from the Seattle Central Community College on Capital Hill (marked with
an X in a circle) and one from Victor Steinbrueck Park, at Elliot Bay by
Pike Place Market (marked with a circle at the bottom of the map). The
labor march route is marked with a line with arrows around pie slice "K".
The heavy lines with short diagonal crosses around the WTO/Convention
Center mark a guess of where police might set up their lines. The
Convergence Center at 420 Denny, is marked with "420," in Pie slice "B."*

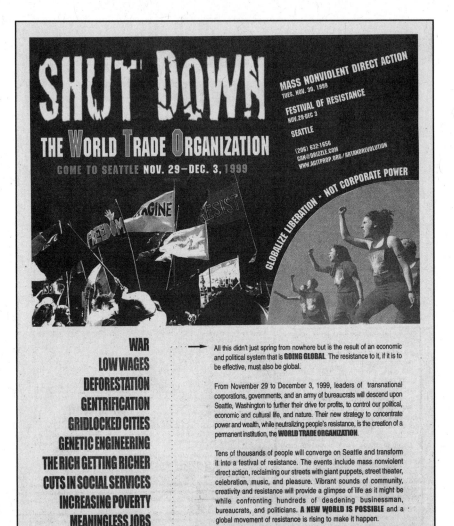

*Front page of the 1999 DIRECT ACTION NETWORK broadsheet.*

The following four articles are reprinted from the October 1999 Direct Action Network (Against Corporate Globalization) four page, two-color newsprint broadsheet/paper. 25,000 copies were printed and distributed, including as an insert to the *Earth First! Journal*, to outreach, mobilize and educate. In addition to these articles, information on local organizing and plans for Seattle anti-WTO events were included.

# Why come to seattle?

By Stephanie Guilloud

*Reprinted from the DAN Broadsheet*

We eat food. ✦ The WTO regulates the standards by which our food is grown, processed, and sold to us. The WTO determines the labor and environmental practices that determine how our food is grown.

We work. ✦ The WTO sets the standards by which employers determine who to hire, how much to pay, what kind of benefits we receive, and the safety conditions of our workplace.

We breathe. ✦ The WTO has already ruled that breathing clean air is not a priority. Higher profits for oil companies is far more important to the benefit of the world.

We go to school. ✦ The WTO wants to create educational standards that limit public sector educational services to the standards that businesspeople and corporations decide. Math programs designed by M&M Candies (what's the chance of a green one?) have already entered our school systems.

We live ✦ in an industrialized country that exploits other nations and other peoples for the sake of comfortable living conditions in the US. We have a responsibility to understand the reality of the global economy beyond our own lives and speak out against these policies. Seattle offers an amazing opportunity to stand together as human beings and declare our sovereignty. Making these connections is the necessary step in creating institutions for our own communities, our needs, our children, and ourselves.

*Artwork by Asante Riverwind used for posters, t-shirts, and "corporate cash."*

# Globalize Liberation, Not Corporate Power

A Call to Action

*Reprinted from the DAN Broadsheet*

RESIST THE WORLD TRADE ORGANIZATION

COME TO SEATTLE NOV. 29–DEC. 3, 1999

FESTIVAL OF RESISTANCE * NONVIOLENT DIRECT ACTION *
STREET THEATER

Increasing poverty and cuts in social services while the rich get richer; low wages, sweatshops, meaningless jobs, and more prisons; deforestation, gridlocked cities and global warming; genetic engineering, gentrification and war: Despite the apparent diversity of these social and ecological troubles, their roots are the same—a global economic system based on the exploitation of people and the planet.

From Nov. 29 to Dec. 3 in Seattle, WA, thousands of leaders of transnational corporations, government officials and an army of bureaucrats will come to the World Trade Organization's Summit to further their drive for profits, and their control over our political, economic and cultural life, along with the environment. Their new strategy to concentrate power and wealth, while neutralizing people's resistance, is called "economic globalization" and "free trade." But these words just disguise the poverty, misery and ecological destruction of this system.

Tens of thousands of people will converge on Seattle and transform it into a festival of resistance: mass nonviolent direct action; reclaim the streets with giant street theater, puppets, celebration, music, street parties and pleasure; vibrant sounds of community, creativity and resistance and glimpses of life as it could be in the face of hundreds of deadening businessman, bureaucrats and politicians. A new world is possible and a global movement of resistance is rising to make it happen. Imagine replacing the existing social order with a just, free and ecological order based on mutual aid and voluntary cooperation.

Join us. Come to Seattle.

## NOV 30 SHUT DOWN THE WTO

## MASS NONVIOLENT DIRECT ACTION INFO

We are planning a large scale, well organized, high visibility action to SHUT DOWN the World Trade Organization on Tuesday November 30. The World Trade Organization has no right to make undemocratic, unaccountable destructive decisions about our lives, our communities and the earth. We will nonviolently and creatively block them from meeting. Hundreds of people will risk arrest, reflecting the diversity of groups and communities impacted by the WTO and corporate globalization. We envision colorful and festive actions with large-scale street theater as a major element. We will make space and encourage mutual respect for a variety of nonviolent action styles reflecting our different groups and communities. The WTO Summit offers a historic opportunity to halt corporate globalization and to help catalyze a widespread mass movement in North America.

## WHY NONVIOLENT DIRECT ACTION AND STREET THEATER?

It is time to raise the social and political cost to those who aim to increase the destruction and misery caused by corporate globalization, as movements in other parts of the world have. Nonviolent direct action can force corporate globalization onto the front burner of public discussion and, coupled with high visibility street theater, will get national and international alternative and mainstream media coverage. The time is ripe for massive nonviolent direct action against the World Trade Organization (WTO) and the corporate globalization it serves. Demonstrations and protest have been an essential part of every successful social change movement in North American history, but they are too often marginalized by corporate media, too easily dismissed by those we want to engage, and bore participants. Street theater used as a tool for making social change can break into people's consciousness, communicate powerfully and capture the imagination of participants and observers. Well-planned nonviolent direct action can intervene into a process that we have been left out of, showing the depth of our opposition and forcing the issues onto the public agenda. There is an incredible opportunity to use street theater—art, dance, music, giant puppets, graffiti art and theater—and nonviolent direct action to simplify and dramatize the issues of corporate globalization and to develop and spread new and creative forms resistance. This will help catalyze desperately needed mass movements in the US and Canada capable of challenging global capital and making radical change and social revolution.

## DIRECT ACTION NETWORK (AGAINST CORPORATE GLOBALIZATION)

The Direct Action Network is a network of local grassroots groups and street theater groups across the Western United States and Canada who are mobilizing our communities to creatively resist the World Trade Organization and corporate globalization.

**WTO Radical Cheerlead:**

They're trying to take control to do as the please

Globalizing power for their corporate sleaze

WTO, your plan has got to go

Your scheming system we are gonna overthrow

(*everyone shout:*) Take back the power! End corporate greed!

Well there's poverty and misery all over the land

The situation's gotten out of hand

When so few own so much it's time to take a stand

(*everyone shout:*) Take back the power! End corporate greed!

# STOP CORPORATE

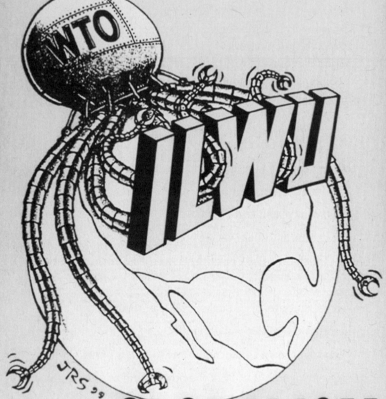

# GLOBALISM

International Longshore and Warehouse Union/ Inlandboatmen's Union of the Pacific

# What is the WTO?

By Stephanie Guilloud and Chris Dixon, August 1999

*Reprinted from the DAN Broadsheet*

---

The World Trade Organization (WTO) is a baby in the era of multinational corporations and international economic agreements. But it's got a big family. The WTO came into being in 1995 as the successor to the General Agreement on Tariffs and Trade (GATT). GATT was established in the wake of the Second World War as a limited set of rules regulating the trade of goods and merchandise among its member nations. Since 1986, GATT has become even more aggressive, though, raising corporations to equal standing with nations and overruling federal, state, and local laws when they "interfere with free trade." The overall goal is to eliminate "trade barriers," frequently including labor laws, public health regulations, and environmental protection measures-all of which get in the way of the corporate bottom-line: profit.

Previously, global agreements like GATT have been temporary and suggestive ideas for international trade regulations. As a child of GATT, however, the WTO solidifies suggested policy into permanent enforced standards. And although the WTO includes 134 member countries, developed nations like the US, Canada, Japan, and those of the European Union repeatedly make key decisions in closed meetings. Meanwhile, in its "dispute resolution system," the WTO allows countries to challenge each other's laws as violations of WTO rules. Cases are decided in secret by a panel of three professional trade bureaucrats (often corporate heads) that aren't bound by any "conflict of interest" rules. It is no surprise, then, that every single environmental or public health law ever challenged at the WTO has been ruled illegal.

Once such a final ruling is issued, losing countries have a set time to make one of three choices: (1) change their law to conform to the WTO requirements, (2) pay compensation to the winning country, or (3) face non-negotiated trade sanctions. In short, what the WTO says goes.

The WTO's decision-making power covers more than traditional trade issues, too. WTO negotiations affect not only goods but also the import and export of services. For instance, privatized educational systems like classes on the web, corporate-owned and operated universities, and study abroad programs are all considered "services." The WTO creates standards that demand the lowest common denominator, which endangers the autonomy and innovation of the public sector.

In addition, the WTO regulates "intellectual property," allowing the patenting of seeds and indigenous knowledge. Officially, the WTO upholds the Trade-Related Intellectual Property Rights Agreement (TRIPs), which mainly benefits Western drug and biotechnology corporations. What this means is that such corporations, protected (and encouraged) by the TRIPs treaty and the WTO, can gather up traditional knowledge of herbs, seeds, medicinal plants, and so on, exercise complete control over any new extensions of that knowledge, and reap the profits. Most people call this theft; the WTO calls it "intellectual property rights." All the while, without the power and money of multinational corporations, the people who lose out—indigenous peoples, as well as many so-called "Third World Countries"—are barely able to fight in ongoing TRIPs disputes, or even enter into debates over Intellectual Property Rights agreements.

Moreover, WTO negotiations deeply affect the environment. For example, in the upcoming November Ministerial, the US government has proposed that a zero-tariff forestry and wood products agreement be signed. This agreement would accelerate the importing and exporting of logs, countering current efforts to protect forests as eco-systems and climate controls. In one swoop, then, it would mean the end for many environmental regulations and other controls on timber production and trade.

Altogether, the main goal of the WTO is to create a fully-integrated global capitalist economy "free" of any "discriminatory" barriers. "Non-discrimination" is a catch word indicating policies that reject any and all obstacles to trade. Case studies, however, illustrate who is actually discriminated against.

THE BEEF HORMONE CASE: After studies in Europe concluded that artificial growth hormones in beef created early menstruation in young girls and health problems, the European Union (EU) banned the sale of beef from cattle that had been raised in this way. In 1998, a WTO panel, called to action by US beef companies, ruled against the law that the EU passed. The EU had until May 13, 1999 to open its markets to hormone-treated beef. Because the EU refuses to open its markets, the WTO forces them to pay upwards of $124 million annually in compensation to the United States.

THE SEA TURTLE CASE: Four Asian nations challenged provisions of the US Endangered Species Act forbidding the sale of shrimp caught in ways that kill endangered sea turtles. In 1998, the WTO ruled that the US was not acting in compliance of WTO rules. Requiring shrimp nets to be fitted with inexpensive "turtle excluder devices" has been ruled "WTO-illegal."

THE CLEAN AIR CASE: On behalf of its oil industry, Venezuela challenged the US Clean Air Act regulation that required gas refiners to produce cleaner gas. A WTO panel ruled against the US law. Foreign oil refiners now have an option to sell dirtier gasoline in the US as a result, despite domestic challenges.

The WTO has the absolute authority to supersede local, state, and even national laws if a corporation pressures its government to challenge a particular mandate. Without any avenues of accountability and very few avenues of transparency, anyone who is not a corporate head, trade official, or WTO bureaucrat is effectively shut out of all decisions. Clearly, THE WTO IS NOT OUR INSTITUTION. We do not control its process, and we do not benefit from its decisions.

## WTO IN SEATTLE

Seattle, Washington is touted as a major gateway to the markets of Asia and, particularly, Japan. According to the Seattle Host Organization for the WTO (headed up by Bill Gates of Microsoft and Phil Conduit of Boeing) one in four jobs in Washington state are directly related to exports.

The November 29–December 3 WTO Ministerial Meeting is the first trade meeting of its kind to be held on US soil. When similar negotiations take place in Singapore, the Philippines, Geneva, and other places worldwide, the opposition gathers in the hundreds of thousands.

The magnitude of this meeting is far greater than the 6,000 delegates from 135 countries that will attend. Indeed, the WTO meeting will transform Seattle into a militarized zone. Roads will be blocked, the police are prepped for riot response, and SWAT teams are "flexible." Our presence in Seattle demands attention to the growing global economy and its effects on the natural world, working people, Southern nations, and indigenous peoples around the world. Our presence in Seattle demands public space as a non-negotiable right. The affront of the WTO meeting represents a challenge to connect all of us as workers for a more just and livable world.

*Sources:*

"A Citizen's Guide to the World Trade Organization." APEX Press, 1999.

Shiva, Vandana. *Biopiracy.* South End, 1997.

*The Case Against the Global Economy.* Sierra Club, 1996.

# Global Resistance

By Chris Borte

*Reprinted from the DAN Broadsheet*

Resistance to the WTO is growing daily. People are organizing from the ground up and forming alliances worldwide among grassroots labor, environmental, and social justice groups to oppose this neoliberal institution: Teachers hunger striking against privatization in Argentina, working side by side with women organizing against quasi-slavery in the "Maquila" factories of Mexico, Bangladesh, Salvador, and Nicaragua; farmers struggling against globalization in India, Philippines, Brazil, Estonia, Norway, Honduras, France, Spain, Switzerland, Bangladesh, Senegal, Mozambique, Togo, Peru, Bolivia, Columbia and many other countries; Ogoni, Maori, Maya, Aymara, U'wa and other indigenous peoples fighting for their cultural rights and physical survival; students struggling against nuclear power or the repression of striking workers in Ukraine and South Korea; rank and file labor like postal workers from Canada resisting privatization, women's rights activists, environmentalists, unemployed, fisher folk, anti-racists, peace mobilizers, and animal rights activists...the list could easily fill these pages.

Coalitions that formed to oppose NAFTA, GATT, APEC, and the Multinational Agreement on Investment (MAI) have grown more experienced and successful at working together to fight corporate globalization. Forging those necessary links between our movements becomes far easier when we realize the assholes who are clear-cutting the last of our ancient forests are the same assholes who are trying to smash our unions and destroy the limited forms of democratic control we still have. The old 1960s slogan "think globally, act locally" is no longer sufficient. We must create ways of thinking and acting both locally and globally at the same time.

One of the most exciting movements fighting corporate globalization formed in February of 1998, when peoples' movements from all continents met in Geneva and launched a worldwide coordination of resistance called Peoples' Global Action Against "Free" Trade and the

World Trade Organization (PGA). In their literature they emphasize four major points: (1) A very clear rejection of the WTO and other neoliberal trade agreements as active promoters of a socially and environmentally destructive globalization; (2) A confrontational attitude, since we do not think that lobbying can have a major impact in such biased and undemocratic organizations, in which transnational capital is the only real policy-maker; (3) A call to non-violent civil disobedience and the construction of local alternatives by local people as answers to the action of governments and corporations; (4) An organizational philosophy based on decentralization and autonomy.

PGA intends to serve as a global instrument for communication and co-ordination for all those fighting against the destruction of humanity and the planet by the global market, as well as building up local alternatives and peoples' power. Their first call to action was the June 18th protests against the G8 summit in Germany. Movements ranging from the Chikoko Movement in Nigeria to the Pakistani trade unions, from the Argentinean churches to a broad coalition of social movements in London, occupied the financial centers of their cities to reject the rule of the G8. Such coordinated resistance in a total of 41 countries showed that the process of converging our movements is gaining strength and speed. Even as this article goes to press, PGA is organizing at their second conference in Bangalore, India for the WTO meeting in Seattle and beyond.

## "NOT PEPSI/COKE, WE WANT WATER!"

"Not Pepsi/Coke, we want water," cries the National Alliance of People's Movements in India. They are calling for India to quit the WTO and campaign for an alternative institution to regulate world-trade in a democratic, pro-people and environmentally sustainable way. They believe all transnational corporations (TNC) should be forced out of India and have called for a boycott on all TNC goods.

This is in stark contrast with those who hold hope of achieving justice through reforming the WTO. Reforms lead nowhere when corporations and their governmental counterparts are in charge. We need to globalize solidarity and liberation, not capitalism, and fight for a participatory and sustainable global village. The WTO must be shut down.

Over the past two decades, people's movements have waged successful campaigns against the operations of transnational corporations on numerous fronts ranging from worldwide boycotts against Nestlé on infant formula, bank loans to South Africa, the battles against Union Carbide over the Bhopal disaster in India, the repression of Coca-Cola workers in Guatemala, the promotion of bio-tech milk products by chemical companies like Monsanto, and the clear-cut logging and deforestation by Mitsubishi and MacMillan Bloedel, to name but a few. It is important to remember that these corporations do not have infinite power—they are not inevitable. We live in a concrete world, within time and space, with ongoing processes that we can affect. We can shut down these bastards.

Just a few years ago it may have seemed impossible to stop the Multilateral Agreement on Investment, a trade agreement that would have given corporations the authority to sue countries for policies that placed people or the environment over profits. And yet due to movements like those mentioned in this article the MAI was shut down. WTO, you're next! ❧

*Photo by Jacob Henifin.*

# Contributor Biographies

**Anuradha Mittal** is the founder and executive director of the Oakland Institute, a leading think-tank on global social, economic, and environmental rights issues, which works with a grassroots constituency to strengthen popular struggles nationally and internationally (www.oaklandinstitute.org). A native of India, Anuradha is an expert on trade, development, human rights, and agriculture issues. She is the author and editor of numerous publications, including her most recent book, *Voices From Africa: African Farmers & Environmentalists Speak Out Against a New Green Revolution in Africa.*

**David Solnit** lived and organized in Seattle in 1999 with the Direct Action Network, a group co-initiated by the Art and Revolution Collective, of which he was a part. He has been a mass direct action organizer since the early '80s, and in the '90s became a puppeteer and arts organizer. He is the editor of *Globalize Liberation: How to Uproot the System and Build a Better World* and co-author with Aimee Allison of *Army of None; Strategies to Counter Military Recruitment, End War and Build a Better World.* He currently works as a carpenter in Oakland, California and organizes with Courage to Resist, supporting GI resisters, and with the Mobilization for Climate Justice West.

**Rebecca Solnit** is an activist, historian and writer who lives in San Francisco. Her twelfth book, *A Paradise Built in Hell: The Extraordinary Communities that Arise in Disaster,* came out this fall. The previous eleven include 2007's *Storming the Gates of Paradise; A Field Guide to Getting Lost; Hope in the Dark: Untold Histories, Wild Possibilities; Wanderlust: A History of Walking; As Eve Said to the Serpent: On Landscape, Gender and Art; River of Shadows, Eadweard Muybridge and the Technological Wild West* (for which she received a Guggenheim, the National Book Critics Circle Award in criticism, and the Lannan Literary Award). A contributing editor to *Harper's,* she frequently writes for the political site Tomdispatch.com. She has worked on antinuclear, antiwar, environmental, indigenous land rights and human rights campaigns and movements over the years.

**Chris Dixon,** originally from Alaska, is a longtime anarchist organizer, writer, and educator, and a PhD candidate in the History of Consciousness program at the University of California at Santa Cruz. During the late 1990s, he was a student activist at the Evergreen State College in Olympia, Washington. In 1999, Dixon helped launch the Direct Action Network and was deeply involved in organizing for the protests against the Seattle WTO ministerial. He is currently completing a book based on interviews with radical organizers across the US and Canada focusing on anti-authoritarian politics in broader-based movements. Dixon serves on the advisory board for the activist journal *Upping the Anti* and lives in Sudbury, Ontario, Atikameksheng Anishnawbek Territory, where he is involved with anti-war and Indigenous solidarity organizing. Contact him at chrisd@resist.ca.

**Stephanie Guilloud** was a key organizer of the Seattle WTO shutdown with the Direct Action Network. She edited an anthology of first-hand accounts called *Voices from the WTO.* Currently Stephanie is an organizer with Project South in Atlanta, and works closely with Southerners On New Ground (SONG). She worked on local, regional, and national planning committees to organize the 2007 United States Social Forum.

**Chris Borte** organized with the Direct Action Network and Portland Jobs With Justice. He mobilized Portland folks to the WTO protests and participated in the shutdown of the WTO with the Key Lime Cluster. He co-founded Portland Art and Revolution, and has been a tenant and community organizer. He still hates capitalism, loves democracy, and supports his partner Amy in her work as co-director of Rural Organizing Project doing rural, radical statewide organizing using a small group democracy model.

# Support AK Press!

AK Press is one of the world's largest and most productive anarchist publishing houses. We're entirely worker-run and democratically managed. We operate without a corporate structure—no boss, no managers, no bullshit. We publish close to twenty books every year, and distribute thousands of other titles published by other like-minded independent presses from around the globe.

The Friends of AK program is a way that you can directly contribute to the continued existence of AK Press, and ensure that we're able to keep publishing great books just like this one! Friends pay a minimum of $25 per month, for a minimum three month period, into our publishing account. In return, Friends automatically receive (for the duration of their membership), as they appear, one free copy of every new AK Press title. They're also entitled to a 20% discount on everything featured in the AK Press Distribution catalog and on the website, on any and every order. You or your organization can even sponsor an entire book if you should so choose!

There's great stuff in the works—so sign up now to become a Friend of AK Press, and let the presses roll!

Won't you be our friend? Email friendsofak@akpress.org for more info, or visit http://www.akpress.org/programs/friendsofak